★ ★ ★ ★ ★ ★

Learn some hands-on history!

Great Colonial America Projects

You Can Build Yourself!

Kris Bordessa

nomad press

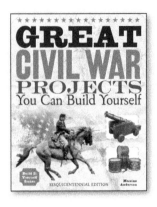
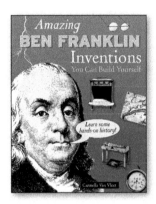

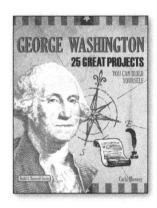

Nomad Press
A division of Nomad Communications
10 9 8 7 6 5 4

ISBN: 978-0-97712-940-9

Educational Consultant, Marla Conn

Questions regarding the ordering of this book should be addressed to

Nomad Press
2456 Christian St.
White River Junction, VT 05001
www.nomadpress.net

Image Credits: p. viii, John Smith map: wikipedia; p. x, map of colonial North America: www.loc.gov; p. 56, mobcap: www.probertencyclopedia.com; p. 57, gentlemen: www.costumes.org; p. 70, woman working: www2.world66.com; p. 71, old Philadelphia map: www.loc.gov; p. 82, Cotton Mather: www.loc.gov; p. 83, Ben Franklin: www.photolib.noaa.gov ; p. 87, Witch Trials: wikipedia.org; p. 94, cipher: courtesy of the NSA; p. 99 printing press: www.fromoldbooks.org
Courtesy of Historic Deerfield, Inc.: p. 42, clothing; p. 51, pocket; p. 60, footwear; p. 70, cook; p. 86, barometer; p. 88, firebucket.
Illustrations by Shawn Braley: p. v, clipper ship; p. 1, colonists sailing; p. 14, Fort Necessity; p. 15, firing line; p. 20, planting; p. 24, Pocahontas; p. 25, house; p. 26, privy; p. 27, wattle and daub; p. 30, bed; p. 38, laundry by fire; p. 41, colonists; p.45, woman spinning; p. 67, Eliza Lucas; p. 72, mansion; p. 88, pillory; p. 101, bookbinder; p. 105, child; p. 109, school scene.
Illustrations by Jeff McAllister: p. 12, farm workers; p. 21, wampum; p. 33, dipping candles; p. 44, Daniel Boone; p. 48, weaver at loom; p. 59, woman with fan.

Contents

UNITE OR DIE

Introduction

Imagine stepping aboard a creaking wooden ship with billowing sails. You are about to begin a trip across the Atlantic Ocean from Europe to an unnamed land. You'll toss and turn in rough seas for months and months. During the trip, there will be no way to contact any of your loved ones.

Well, that's exactly what some brave men and women did in the sixteenth, seventeenth, and eighteenth centuries. They left their homes—and in many cases members of their family—to settle a new land, as foreign to them as Mars is to you. These men and women followed in the footsteps of some famous explorers, traveling to the land we know now as the United States of America. They started a new life that would forever change our world.

This book will help you to understand a little about what life was like for the colonists who journeyed to this new land. You will discover why those people chose to make such a bold move. You'll understand how they lived and learn some interesting facts about famous—and not-so-famous—colonists. You will also create some projects that will help show you how the colonists survived, entertained themselves, dressed, and communicated. You'll learn about life in a colonial home and in a colonial town, and about colonial craftspeople and colonial law and order.

Most of the projects in this book can be made by kids with minimal adult supervision, and the supplies needed are either common household items or easily available at craft stores. So, take a step back into colonial America and get ready to **Build it Yourself**.

Colonial America Timeline and An Overview of the Thirteen Colonies

The 13 original colonies developed over many years. People in Europe ruled the colonies, and communication between them and the colonists who actually lived on the land was sometimes vague. This often caused confusion about who owned what land. Below you'll find a brief look at each colony and how it began. Remember that this is by no means a complete list of everything that happened in each colony!

★ 1600s

1606 King James I grants a charter to the Virginia Company

1608 First women arrive in Jamestown

1609 Captain John Smith is burned in a keg powder accident and returns to England

1614 John Rolfe marries Rebecca (Pocahontas)

1614 Captain John Smith returns to the colonies and maps the Massachusetts Bay area

1618 The Virginia Company creates the House of Burgesses

Virginia

- In 1607, the Virginia Company settles in Jamestown, named for England's King James I
- From 1609 to 1610, Jamestown's population shrinks from 550 people to only 65, during what became known as the Starving Time
- Virginia becomes a royal colony in 1624

New York

- The Dutch West India Company explores the area as early as 1614
- New Amsterdam is settled on what is now Manhattan Island (collectively, the Dutch holdings in this area were called New Netherlands)
- In 1664, King Charles II reclaims the territory and grants it to his brother, the duke of York, who renames the colony New York
- New York becomes a royal colony in 1685

Massachusetts

- The Pilgrims arrive on the *Mayflower* in 1620 and settle in Plymouth
- John Winthrop, with the Massachusetts Bay charter, arrives in 1630 and founds Boston and the Massachusetts Bay Company
- Massachusetts becomes a royal colony in 1691

1619 First African settlers brought to Jamestown

1634 Anne Hutchinson, one of the founders of Rhode Island, arrives in the colonies

1636 Harvard College is founded in Cambridge, Massachusetts

New Hampshire

- During the 1620s there are several grants by the English crown for the area that is now New Hampshire and Vermont, and the first settlers found a fishing and trading settlement
- The name of New Hampshire is given to what is now southern New Hampshire in 1629
- The Massachusetts Bay colony administers the entire region, including what is now Maine, from 1641 until New Hampshire becomes a royal colony in 1679

Maryland

- Lord Baltimore is granted a charter in 1632
- The first settlers reach Maryland in 1634
- Maryland becomes a royal colony in 1692, and remains so until 1715, when Charles Calvert, the fifth Lord Baltimore, regains control of the colony

Connecticut

- As early as 1633, Dutch traders settle near Hartford
- In 1636, Thomas Hooker, a clergyman who has been driven out of Massachusetts, arrives in Hartford
- In 1662, a royal charter is granted to John Winthrop, Jr.

1639 Richard Fairbanks's tavern in Boston becomes the first official colonial post office for overseas mail

1641 Massachusetts becomes the first colony to recognize slavery

1643 Evangelista Torrecelli invents the mercury barometer

1643 Anne Hutchinson killed

Delaware

- Under a grant from the New Sweden Company, Peter Minuet leads Swedish settlers to the Delaware area in 1638
- In 1655 the Dutch gain control of the area
- The English battle the Dutch for control of Delaware and finally gain control in 1674
- Delaware becomes an independent colony in 1701, electing its own assembly in 1704

1664 English take control of Dutch colonies

1683 Pennsylvania's first post office opens

1692 Salem Witch Trials

1693 College of William and Mary is founded in Virginia

1699 No woolens can be exported from any colony as part of the Navigation Acts

Rhode Island

- In 1636, Roger Williams, who has been run out of Massachusetts for his religious and political beliefs, buys an area of land from the Native Americans in the area now called Providence
- In 1638, Anne Hutchinson and some of her followers settle an area near Newport, Rhode Island
- In 1663, King Charles II grants a charter to Williams

1648 Peter Stuyvesant appoints first fire wardens in New Amsterdam (New York)

1650 England forbids trade between foreign ships and the colonies as part of the Navigation Acts

North Carolina

- The area is explored and briefly settled by the Spanish in the 1500s
- Between 1585 and 1587 Sir Walter Raleigh unsuccessfully attempts to establish a colony on Roanoke Island off the coast of present-day North Carolina
- In 1653, Virginia colonists begin to expand into the North Carolina region
- In 1663, King Charles II grants eight of his supporters a charter for the area covering what is now North Carolina, South Carolina, and Georgia, known as the Carolina grant
- The designation of North Carolina is first used in 1691, when it is recognized by the crown
- North Carolina becomes a royal colony in 1729

★1700s

1704 The *Boston News-Letter* is first published

1706 Benjamin Franklin is born

1732 George Washington is born

1733 Benjamin Franklin first publishes *Poor Richard's Almanack*

1737 Benjamin Franklin appointed postmaster of Philadelphia

South Carolina

- In 1663, King Charles II grants eight of his supporters a charter for the area covering what is now North Carolina, South Carolina, and Georgia
- Colonists settle the area that is now Charleston in 1680
- South Carolina splits from North Carolina and becomes a royal colony in 1729

1743 Thomas Jefferson is born

1752 Benjamin Franklin's famous kite-flying experiment

New Jersey

- In 1664, the duke of York receives a patent to the area between the Connecticut and Delaware rivers
- New Jersey is granted to Lord Berkeley and Sir George Carteret by the duke of York, causing confusion about its government
- New Jersey becomes a royal colony in 1702

Pennsylvania

- Pennsylvania is granted to William Penn in 1681
- In 1682, the city of Philadelphia is laid out and becomes a model city plan

1754 French and Indian War begins

1763 End of French and Indian War

Georgia

- Spanish missions and military posts dot the coastline of this area in the 1600s
- Georgia is originally the southern portion of the Carolina grant
- In 1732, King George II grants a charter to James Edward Oglethorpe
- Georgia becomes a royal colony in 1752

1765 The Stamp Act is signed into law

1773 The Boston Tea Party

1775 The Revolutionary War between Britain and the colonies begins

1776 The signing of the Declaration of Independence

Map of North America, 1784.

Chapter 1

How It All Began

Hundreds of years ago, the country we now know as the United States of America was mysterious, wild, and untamed. It had deep forests and rugged terrain. Europeans only knew a little about this new world. They learned about it from bold explorers such as Christopher Columbus and Ponce de León. During the 1400s and 1500s, these early explorers sailed from Europe in search of gold, silk, and spices. They hoped to find an easy route to the **Orient**, where they were sure they would find riches. They did find some of these things, but while they searched, they also discovered parts of the world that were completely new to them. One of those places was the continent of North America.

The explorers who arrived on the shores of this new continent were very curious about it. They anchored their ships and set off on foot hoping to find something valuable—maybe even gold. But those explorers had no idea just how large North America is. They were only able to explore the area along the eastern coast where their ship had dropped them off. In the short time they were on land, they only saw a small portion of the country.

In the southern part of the continent, a Spaniard named Hernán Cortés explored what is now Mexico and did discover gold. He conquered the people there, called the Aztecs, then

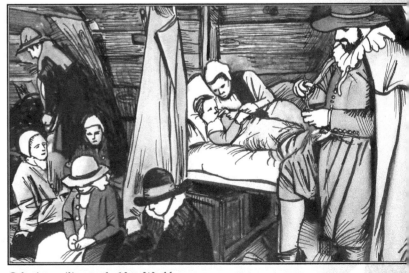

Colonists sailing to the New World.

Columbus discovers the New World.

claimed the land for Spain. Cortés brought treasure back to his homeland and told people about the new world and its riches. Cortés, Columbus, and Ponce de León were among the first Europeans to explore this new land, but they certainly weren't the last.

Word of this new land trickled in to Europe from many different ships returning home to Spain, Portugal, and England. Sailors told of the lands they had explored. Most explorers only partially understood where other explorers had been. Different ships had traveled to different parts of the continent. Stories were passed by word of mouth as people traveled. As stories usually do, the tales grew grander as they were passed along. Many stories said that gold was plentiful, and with only a little work, a person could make a fortune.

The New World

In 1584, Queen Elizabeth I of England gave Sir Walter Raleigh permission to **colonize** America. One hundred men sailed to the New World in 1585 and formed the first English **colony**. They landed on an island off the coast of present-day North Carolina, and named it Roanoke. These colonists were not prepared for life in the New World. They didn't have enough supplies, and they didn't get along with their Native American neighbors. Their supply ship from England was delayed, leaving them short on food. The colonists became hungry, and desperate. When an unexpected explorer named Sir Francis Drake showed up at Roanoke, the settlers abandoned the colony and returned to England aboard Drake's ship.

Many stories said that gold was plentiful, and with only a little work, a person could make a fortune.

Sir Walter Raleigh wasn't ready to give up. He was determined to colonize the New World, so he sent a second group across the Atlantic in 1587. Thirty-seven days after the colonists arrived at Roanoke, their governor, John White, returned to England for supplies.

Sir Walter Raleigh

But a war broke out between England and Spain, and he couldn't sail back to the Roanoke colony for almost three years. When he did finally return, White found the colony empty. A single word—Croatoan—was carved into a post. White suspected that this was a sign that the colonists had moved to Croatoan Island, but when he went to the island he couldn't find a trace of the colonists. No one ever found the missing colonists. The fate of the lost colony of Roanoke remains one of the great mysteries of American history.

In 1606, England's King James I granted a **charter** to a group of 214 men who called themselves the Virginia Company. This group's plan was to settle in the **New World**. Like others before them, they hoped to find gold and a water route to the Orient. After five long months at sea, they arrived at Jamestown Island off the coast of Virginia on May 14, 1607. These men were really unprepared to live in the New World. The land was rugged and covered with forests of large trees—nothing like London. The colonists had to cut down trees, build shelters, and prepare the land for planting.

The Powhatans

The Powhatan Indian tribe was part of the Algonquian nation. The Powhatan leader was Wahunsenacawh, but Powhatan was his common name. Chief Powhatan inherited six tribes that lived near present-day Richmond, Virginia. Powhatan ruled 30 tribes at the peak of his leadership. Each tribe was governed by a werowance, a leader who was faithful to Powhatan. These leaders paid **tribute** to Powhatan, making him a wealthy man. He was able to take care of a large family—he had more than 100 wives! One of Powhatan's daughters, Matoaka, was nicknamed Pocahontas, meaning "playful one."

The Powhatan people lived in villages made of dome-shaped homes. Each home had a large garden area where the Powhatans grew corn, beans, peas, squash, pumpkins, and sunflowers. These homegrown foods were important, but the Powhatans also depended on hunting, fishing, and gathering wild foods for much of their diet.

Colonial Words to Know

the Orient: the East, as in Asia

colonize: to establish a colony

colony: a settlement in a foreign place

charter: permission from the king, allowing a group to settle a portion of land and govern it as the group sees fit

New World: the continents of North and South America

tribute: a sum of money or other valuable thing paid by one ruler or nation to another in submission, as the price of peace and protection

Captain John Smith

Captain John Smith was a member of the Virginia Company that first settled in Jamestown. He had strong beliefs about how to do things, and sometimes he offended or angered people. In fact, Smith's shipmates accused him of planning to overthrow the colony's leaders and put him in prison on the ship during their voyage to the New World. They dropped the charges against Smith when they landed, and he was one of seven men chosen to be part of the governing council of Virginia. When some of the colonists argued over the shortage of supplies and the laziness of some of the group, Smith went looking for a solution. He left the colony to explore the Chesapeake Bay region and search for food.

When Smith came back, he became president of the colony. His strict leadership made some members of the colony dislike him. But his harsh policies, including his proclamation that "He who does not work, will not eat," helped the settlement survive and begin to thrive. Smith was badly burned in a gunpowder accident in 1609 and traveled to England for medical treatment. He returned to the colonies for a short period in 1614 to explore the Massachusetts Bay area, where he coined the term "New England."

John Smith was stubborn. He didn't like to follow orders from England when he was in the New World. When Smith went back to England for a visit, the English government would not let him return to the colonies. He spent the rest of his life in London writing books. Smith died at age 51.

Many of these first colonists were gentlemen who were used to the comforts of England. They were not very good at taming the wilderness, but they did their best to make the colony succeed. The men had to work very hard just to survive in this new wild land. It didn't leave much opportunity or time for treasure hunting. They quickly learned that the stories were a bit exaggerated anyway! They didn't find gold scattered along the ground as they had hoped. Because they weren't used to working so hard or living in such a rugged place, some of the men became grouchy and impatient.

The Jamestown fort.

The Jamestown settlers built a fort to protect themselves from attacks by the native Algonquian people. But the fort didn't protect them from disease and hunger—within two years, only 60 of the original 214 settlers remained. The rest had died.

While there were some conflicts between the Algonquian people and the Virginia Company, eventually they both realized that a peaceful relationship would be better than a violent one. The colony began trading with the Powhatan Indian tribes, which were part of the Algonquian nation. The Powhatan tribe traded food for the copper and iron tools that the colonists had brought from Europe. But even with the kindness of these native people, life was difficult and the colonists ran low on supplies. By June 1609, the Jamestown colonists decided to abandon the town. Just as they were about to leave,

The Pilgrims who came to the New World on the *Mayflower* traveled 2,700 miles over the open ocean at a rate of 2 miles per hour. You could travel faster on your skateboard or bike!

though, supply ships arrived with food, and they changed their minds. Jamestown went on to become the first permanent British colony in the New World.

The *Mayflower* Voyage

While the *Mayflower* didn't bring the first colonists to the New World, its voyage is certainly the most famous.

The travelers on the *Mayflower* wanted to leave Europe to find religious freedom. They were **Puritans** who called themselves Separatists, because they wanted to separate from the official Church of England. We call them Pilgrims because they came to the New World on a religious pilgrimage, or quest. When King James would not allow them to start a church of their own in England, the Separatists moved to Holland in 1608, where religious freedom was accepted. But they missed the English life and familiar customs. When their children began speaking Dutch and forgetting English ways, the Separatists knew it was time to move. The group worked out a plan to move their church to the New World.

Colonial Words to Know

Puritans: a group of Protestant Christians in England who were persecuted for their beliefs

pallet: a straw mattress or bedding spread on the floor

hammock: a swinging netting or canvas supported by cords from supports at each end

shallot: the small boat on a ship used to ferry people to land

chamber pot: a container used indoors as a toilet

The *Mayflower* started from England with another ship—the *Speedwell*—in 1620. The *Speedwell* sprung a leak, and both ships turned back. Most of the passengers from the *Speedwell* crowded onto the *Mayflower*, determined to cross the Atlantic Ocean to the New World and a new life.

Talk about crowded! Two ships' worth of passengers squeezed onto one wooden ship. The *Mayflower* carried 102 passengers and about 30 crewmembers. The passengers spent most of their time between decks, where there was almost no privacy. Some passengers made

The Church of England

The Church of England was—and still is—the established church of England. Sometimes called the Anglican Church, it is a Christian church. Between 1529 and 1536, under the reign of King Henry VIII, the Church of England became a national church. This meant that instead of a religious leader being the official head of the church, the king or queen made all religious decisions. As kings and queens ascended to the throne, they brought their religious beliefs with them and expected their subjects to worship accordingly. Can you imagine changing your beliefs to match those of the person on the throne?

Of course, this led to some trouble—having the king or queen in charge of worship made it difficult for people to express their religious beliefs freely. Many people in England were executed simply because their beliefs differed from those of the reigning queen or king. One thing that caused trouble was the bible. Some royalty felt that it should only be written in Latin; others felt that it should be translated into English. If someone owned an English translation of the bible during the reign of a king or queen who insisted only on Latin bibles, it was considered treason and the offender was beheaded! The church went through some changes in the second half of the 1500s as kings and queens came and went, but many groups of people were unhappy with the rituals used in worship and the crown's control of religion. One group, the Separatists, were so sick and tired of royal rulers telling them how they could worship that they moved to the New World. Today, we call them the Pilgrims.

The Mayflower Compact

The Mayflower Compact was written on board the *Mayflower* by Governor William Bradford. The document was signed by all of the men on the *Mayflower*.

Here's what it says:

"In ye name of God, Amen. We whose names are underwritten, the loyall subjects of our dread sovraign Lord, King James, by the grace of God, of Great Britaine, Franc, and Ireland king, defender of the faith, etc.

Haveing undertaken, for ye glorie of God, and advancemente of ye Christian faith, and honour of our king & countrie, a voyage to plant ye first colonie in ye Northerne parts of Virginia, doe by these presents solemnly & mutualy in ye presence of God, and one of another, covenant & combine our selves togeather into a civill body politick, for our better ordering & preservation & furtherance of ye ends aforesaid; and by vertue hearof to enacte lawes, ordinances, acts constitutions, & offices, from time to time, as shall be thought most meet & convenient for ye generall good of ye Colonie, unto which we promise all due submission and obedience. In witnes wherof we have hereunder subscribed our names at Cap-Codd ye 11th. of November, in ye year of ye raigne of our soveraigne lord, King James, of England, France, & Ireland ye eighteenth, and of Scotland, ye fiftie fourth. Ano: Dom. 1620."

curtains to make private space. The travelers slept on **pallets** and in **hammocks**, and some even claimed the **shallop** for their sleeping place.

Passengers were often seasick because the ship tossed and turned. For 66 days the passengers lived together in cramped quarters, where a lack of privacy and fresh water made bathing difficult. **Chamber pots** could only be emptied in good weather—during heavy storms, passengers were forced to stay out of the way of the sailors, no matter how sick they were or how smelly their cramped living quarters became.

When the *Mayflower* reached Cape Cod in Massachusetts, the Pilgrims wrote an agreement called the Mayflower Compact. This became the first

Chamber pot.

self-governing document of the New World. A small group of men went ashore to search for a suitable place to start a colony. Because the *Mayflower* had to turn back to take on the passengers from the *Speedwell*, the Pilgrims began their journey a month later than they had planned. They arrived in the New World on November 21—not long before winter began. As a result, the *Mayflower* was home to many of the Pilgrims during their first winter in the New World. The Pilgrims just could not build enough homes for everyone by the time the first snow began to fall. The Pilgrims suffered through the harsh winter. By winter's end, only half of them were still alive.

The Colonies

As settlers arrived in growing numbers, different colonies began popping up along the East Coast. Each group of settlers brought a different set of traditions and ideas. New York, for example, started out with the name New Amsterdam. It was ruled by the Dutch during the early colonial years. There were also Swedish and French colonies. Settlers in each had their own unique language and way of life. But as settlements formed and time passed, some colonies began to have similarities, regardless of their original customs. This was mostly based upon where they were located. Climate dictated how homes were built and which crops succeeded. Three distinct regions emerged: New England, the Middle Colonies, and the Deep South.

New England was settled quite by accident. The *Mayflower* was headed for Virginia, but storms blew it off course. With passengers ready to **mutiny** (they wanted to get *off* that ship!), they landed at Plymouth Rock rather than search for Virginia.

Eventually, the New England area would include the Massachusetts

Proprietors

Proprietors owned many of the plantations in the Deep South. Many of these men lived in England, while others lived in cities like Savannah or Charleston or further south on the island of Jamaica. A proprietor counted on an overseer to manage the plantation's day-to-day operation. He also counted on slaves for labor. The proprietor came to inspect the plantation several times a year, sometimes staying on during months when mosquitoes—and the disease called malaria that the mosquitoes carried—were not present.

Spotlight on Famous Colonists

William Penn

King Charles II had borrowed a great sum of money from William Penn's father, who was an admiral. When the admiral died, the king repaid the debt to William Penn by giving him a piece of land in the New World. This plot of land was larger than all of England!

Penn was a **Quaker** and wanted to start a colony that accepted the Quaker way of life. But Penn didn't limit who could come—he believed in brotherly love and welcomed anyone into his new colony. William Penn's colony, named Pennsylvania, was different from the other colonies. Because of his Quaker religion, Penn believed in treating people as equals and respecting all religions. Penn lost most of his fortune developing Pennsylvania, but he proved that freedom and fairness work. Philadelphia became the capital of Pennsylvania. It grew to be one of the largest, most prosperous cities in the colonies.

Bay Colony, Connecticut, Rhode Island, and New Hampshire. Boston, part of the Massachusetts Bay Colony, became a shipping hub. Chairs and furniture made in the colony were shipped from Boston. The area's merchants sold textiles to other merchants throughout the colonies. Rhode Island was also involved in the shipping trade, but the colonists there were willing to do the kind of shipping that other colonies weren't—**smuggling** and slave trading.

The Middle Colonies were located around the Hudson and Delaware rivers. These colonies included New York, Delaware, New Jersey, and Pennsylvania. Most of these colonies were originally settled by the Dutch, but the English took control of them in 1664. This area was rich in lumber, with stands of cedar trees (used in making musical instruments) and black locust (desirable for building). There was also much trapping done in the area, so the fur trade thrived.

The colonies in the Deep South, which included Virginia, Maryland, the Carolinas,

37-foot-tall Statue of William Penn atop Philadelphia City Hall.

Colonial Words to Know

mutiny: a revolt against those in charge

smuggling: trading forbidden items

pacifism: the belief that all conflict can be resolved peacefully

Quakers: a group of Christians, also called Religious Society of Friends, who believe in a simple way of life and pacifism

indigo: a plant that yields a blue dye

overseer: a person in charge

Georgia, and even Spanish Florida, were easier to establish than northern colonies. This was probably because, except for Virginia, they were settled later than the earlier colonies. The people who settled these later colonies were able to learn from the mistakes of earlier colonists. The warm southern climate allowed people to experiment with different crops. They tried wine grapes—grapes that would be dried into raisins and currants, various oil-producing crops, and they had much success with tobacco, rice, and **indigo**.

The Triangle Trade

In the late 1600s, a trading route emerged. The triangle began with European ships sailing along the western coast of Africa, trading rum for slaves. These ships brought the slaves to the Caribbean, where some of them were exchanged as field workers for Caribbean sugar and molasses. Next, the European ships brought the Caribbean sugar and molasses—along with the slaves that hadn't been sold—to the colonies where they were traded for tobacco and cotton. With some of the Caribbean sugar, as well as the tobacco and cotton, the ships would head back home to Europe. Due to the triangular pattern of this route, the colonists referred to it as the "triangle trade."

Some slaves were shipped to the colonies from the Caribbean, as part of the triangle trade. Others came to the colonies directly from Africa on what was called the Middle Passage. This difficult ocean crossing could last from 25 to 60 days, and many died during the trip.

People involved in the slave trade saw the captured Africans as nothing more than cargo. With "loose packing," slaves were chained in position side by side on their backs. With "tight packing," they were chained on their sides, nose to toe. Cargo (the slaves) and decks were sometimes washed down only once or twice during the voyage in spite of the human waste and vomit (from seasickness) that surrounded them. Sadly, the cruelty that these enslaved men and women would endure had only just begun.

The land in the south was mostly owned by wealthy men who lived in England. Large farms, called plantations, took the place of towns. **Overseers** managed the day-to-day operation of the plantations, and tradespeople such as coopers and blacksmiths lived and worked on the plantations. Rather than traveling to a town, farmers would visit a nearby plantation when they needed work done by these tradespeople.

It was a huge job to run a plantation. The overseers of plantations became very dependent on slave labor. The slave trade started in the early 1600s. Plantation owners bought men and women who had been captured in Africa and shipped to the New World. These men and women were treated poorly. They were abused by violent overseers who often thought of them as animals. Some slaves were forced to work in the fields under harsh conditions while others worked as household servants. By 1750, 200,000 slaves had been imported from Africa to the southern colonies.

Because of the dangers related to working in the swampy South—alligators, mosquitoes carrying malaria, and water moccasins (poisonous snakes)—many slaves died at a younger age than those working in the north.

Indentured Servants and Slavery

Survival in the New World was hard work. The colonists couldn't do it all by themselves, so they turned to servants for help. Some of these servants were called indentured servants. People became indentured servants when they signed a contract that promised that they would work for a master for a term of 4 to 7 years. Indentured servants commonly worked for no money. Instead, their new master "paid" them by paying for their passage from Europe, along with food, clothing, and shelter once they arrived in the colonies. When the indentured servants completed their term of indenture, they received freedom dues, which often included a piece of land and some of the necessary supplies for survival.

Many indentured servants who came to the New World were convicts, exiled from Britain for grand larceny (theft of any item worth more than a shilling, such as a yard of flannel cloth). Others were middle-class or poor men, women, and children looking for a better life.

Poor living conditions, hard labor, and disease kept many indentured servants from ever seeing freedom—many died before completing their term of service. Indentured servants often ran away from their masters. Because they usually spoke English and were white—as were most of the other colonists—runaway indentured servants were difficult to capture.

The first Africans in the New World arrived in Jamestown in 1619. At first, Africans came to the colonies as indentured servants, a system that was working well in the colonies already. African indentured servants, however, were not given a choice about coming to the colonies; they were forced into service. They were treated just like indentured servants from Britain and worked side by side in the fields with white servants. Like all indentured servants who fulfilled their obligation, they were eventually released from their obligations and became free.

But this posed a problem. Freeing an indentured servant meant that the master was forced to find a replacement worker, and there were few people who could fill this need. Slaves, on the other hand, were a permanent workforce, and African slaves were easy to keep track of because of their skin color. Unlike indentured servants, slaves never

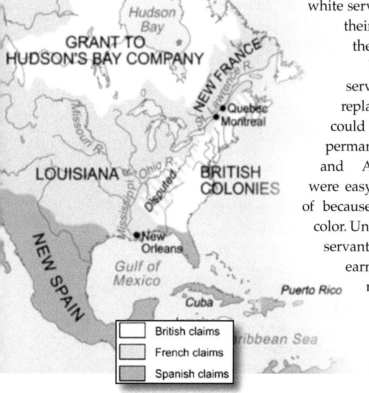

The first Africans in the New World arrived in Jamestown in 1619.

earned freedom. Massachusetts was the first colony to legally recognize slavery, in 1641. In 1662, Virginia proclaimed that all children born to a slave mother would be slaves. This ensured that slavery would be passed from generation to generation, just as skin color was.

GRANT TO HUDSON'S BAY COMPANY

Hudson Bay

NEW FRANCE

Quebec
Montreal

LOUISIANA

Ohio R.

Disputed

Mississippi R.

Missouri R.

BRITISH COLONIES

New Orleans

Gulf of Mexico

NEW SPAIN

Cuba

Puerto Rico

Caribbean Sea

British claims
French claims
Spanish claims

❧ European Influence and Conflict ❧

Between the arrival of the first settlers and the time when all the colonies were ruled by England, there were actually a number of *different* nations trying to control parts of North America. In the seventeenth century, there were Dutch colonies, Swedish colonies, French colonies, and English colonies along the East Coast of North America. The Spanish claimed Florida. And, let's not forget the Native Americans who were here long before any of the colonists.

As Europeans discovered that they could profit from the colonies, countries battled for control of the land. As time passed, the Dutch

Colonial Florida

When we think of colonial America, we often think of the 13 colonies that were ruled by the king of England. But there were other countries interested in the New World as well.

In 1513, Ponce de León, a Spanish explorer, was searching for the Fountain of Youth. The Fountain of Youth was a legendary spring that was supposed to give people who drank from it eternal youth. He did not find the Fountain of Youth, but he did discover the land that we now know as Florida. Ponce de León called the land La Pascua Florida, or "the flowery Easter," because there were so many plants and because his discovery happened during the time of the Spanish Easter feast.

Ponce de León continued searching along the coast of Florida for the Fountain of Youth. He never found it, so he and his crew went to Puerto Rico, where Ponce de León had lived before his explorations. In 1521, Ponce de León returned to Florida with supplies, plans, and settlers to start a colony, but the Native Americans there were not happy to see these settlers. The colonists began building homes on the beach that we now call Sanibel Island. When the angry natives attacked, Ponce de León was struck with an arrow. The colonists left Florida and sailed to the nearest settlement in Cuba where Ponce de León died from his injury. In 1561, another attempt at colonizing Florida was made by a different group, but it too failed.

In 1565, Spaniards finally built their first permanent colony in the New World in St. Augustine, Florida. With St. Augustine as their base, the Spanish began building Catholic missions in the southeastern part of what is now the United States.

The Spanish territory bordered French and English settlements. These countries often had battles over their colonies' boundaries, but the Spanish managed to keep control of the area. In 1763, Spain traded its Florida territory to Great Britain for control of Havana in Cuba.

George Washington

George Washington was born in 1732 in Virginia. Washington was very interested in exploring the unknown area west of the colonies, so at age 16, he helped to survey lands in Virginia's Shenandoah Valley. As a surveyor, he mapped the land, accurately locating property lines, measuring acreage, and noting natural features such as streams and forests.

George Washington became a lieutenant colonel in the British Army (remember, the colonists were primarily British and still governed by British law) and fought in some of the battles that led up to the French and Indian War. At the time, England and France were enemies in the colonies.

George Washington inherited the family home, called Mount Vernon. It had belonged to Washington's father and grandfather before him. Washington remodeled the buildings at Mount Vernon, making it an estate worthy of Virginia's elite colonial society. He devoted himself to managing his land and leading a happy life with his wife, Martha. He became a member of the Virginia House of Burgesses, the first elected lawmaking assembly in the New World. Washington was one of the first prominent colonial men to speak out against England's taxation of the colonies.

As tensions between the colonies and Britain got worse, George Washington commanded all of the colonial military forces. After the Revolutionary War ended in 1783, George Washington returned to a quiet plantation life—until he became the first president of the United States of America in 1789.

Defending Fort Necessity.

conquered the Swedes, and then the English conquered the Dutch. The English expanded their hold in the colonies, eventually taking over Florida in 1763.

France's main interest in the colonies was the fur trade. France was not very interested in colonizing the area; they just wanted to trade with the Native Americans through a network of trading posts along the major rivers. But as the populations in the British colonies grew,

English trappers began intruding on the French fur trade. This made the French angry, and they sent a small force to burn out the village of Native Americans who had been trading furs with the English. In 1753 Virginia's new governor, Robert Dinwiddie, decided to send a small party out to fight off the French. A man named George Washington led that party.

Washington and his troops launched a surprise attack on the Frenchmen. Ten Frenchmen, along with a French commander, were killed. The French claimed that the men were diplomats, coming to Virginia to negotiate. Instead of sensibly retreating, Washington quickly built a stockade he called Fort Necessity. Washington battled the French from Fort Necessity, but one third of his men were killed. He surrendered to the French, who sent Washington and his men home. This event triggered the beginning of the French and Indian War.

In 1754, the British and the Iroquois Confederacy met and made an alliance. Britain provided the Iroquois with weapons and supplies, and the Native Americans helped the British fight against the French for control

What Exactly Is a Colony?

A colony is a piece of land or group of people who belong to or are ruled by a country that is far away. From the time the Jamestown colony began in 1607 until the signing of the Declaration of Independence in 1776, the East Coast of North America was made up mostly of English colonies. Europe was an ocean away, but the people who lived in the colonies were still governed by rulers in those distant lands.

The Iroquois Confederacy

The Iroquois Confederacy was known among Europeans as the League of Five Nations. It originally consisted of the Mohawk, Onondaga, Cayuga, Oneida, and Seneca nations. The members of the Iroquois Confederacy lived in the area that is now central New York. This group of Native Americans was strong and skilled in warfare. They remained independent throughout the colonial period and, with the exception of some of the Mohawk and Cayuga, were allies of the British. They did not want France to expand its colonies southward from Canada and fought alongside the British to prevent this from happening.

of the colonies. After fighting for 9 years, Britain gained control of more than half of the North American continent—and all 13 of the colonies—with the signing of the Treaty of Paris in 1763.

❧ Colonial Law and Order ❧

The British colonists liked the idea of representative government. This is a government in which the citizens have power through elected officials. It was an idea that was becoming popular in England, and in 1618, the Virginia Company created the House of Burgesses, the first such representative assembly in colonial America. Even though the colonists were developing their own ideas about government in the New World, the king of England was still in control over the colonies. In some cases, the king picked the governor of a colony; in other cases, English men owned and managed the colonies. These colonies were called "proprietary colonies" and were governed by the owner of the land. New York, New Jersey, Maryland, Delaware, North Carolina, South Carolina, Pennsylvania, and New Hampshire all started out as proprietary colonies.

Angry colonists.

All but Pennsylvania, Delaware, and Maryland eventually came under the control of the king. These three remained proprietary colonies until they became part of the United States. Virginia, Massachusetts, Rhode Island, and Connecticut were corporate colonies (or charters) and selected their own governors and political leaders, with the king granting permission for those leaders to govern the colony as they saw fit.

The colonies were far, far away from England. At first, the king was content to have little to do with the governing of this land. This allowed self-government to grow and become popular in the colonies. But as the colonies became successful, the king decided he wanted to have control over what was going on there. When he saw that Virginia was thriving, King James I made Virginia the first royal colony. He claimed control over the government of the colony and made the Church of England the official church. This meant that landowners had to pay to support the ministers of the church. Virginia became the model for royal colonies throughout America.

The colonists began to get tired of England ruling their every action. Even though British officials didn't like it, in the early part of the eighteenth century, power began to shift from English-appointed governors and councils to American-elected assemblies. Eventually, the colonists who believed in self-government would stand as one against British soldiers in the Revolutionary War.

The Boston Tea Party

More than 150 years after the first colonists arrived in the New World, they still bought many of their goods from England. When Britain tried to tax many necessities including the lead, glass, paper, paint, and tea delivered to the colonies, the colonists simply refused to buy anything imported from England.

This time, the English merchants got mad. They lost a lot of their business when the colonists stopped ordering from them! The merchants demanded that the taxes be withdrawn, or repealed. In 1770, the king repealed all of the taxes except for the tax on tea.

By 1773, the colonists were getting really tired of King George III and Parliament forcing taxes upon them. Some of the colonists in Boston dressed up as Native Americans and climbed aboard a ship that had arrived in Boston Harbor loaded with English tea. The law stated that if the tea was unloaded onto the docks, the colonists would be required to pay taxes on it. The colonists boarded the ship and dumped the entire load of English tea right into Boston Harbor.

"no taxation without representation"

New
Hampshire

Massachusetts

New
York

Rhode Island

Connecticut

New Jersey

Delaware

Maryland

Pennsylvania

Mississippi
River

Virginia

Ohio
River

North
Carolina

South
Carolina

Atlantic
Ocean

Georgia

Florida

Under
Spanish
Control

Gulf of Mexico

Chapter 2

The First Americans

Explorers who came to North America during the fifteenth and sixteenth centuries found a land that was unclaimed by any European country. They decided that if no European owned the land, it was up for grabs, right? That's how many of these newcomers acted. Europeans made plans to colonize this new land without any concern for the native people already here, their way of life, and their beliefs.

The Native Americans who called North America home lived in harmony with the earth. They understood how to use natural resources without depleting them. While each Native American tribe lived in a certain region, they did not believe that people could own the land. They believed that people were one part of the giant web of life.

The Native Way

Many scientists believe that some of the Native American people descended from people who migrated from Siberia more than 10,000 years ago. These people may have come across the Bering Land Bridge, which is now under water and called the Bering Strait. Historians believe that there were millions of Native Americans living on the North American continent before the first Europeans came, though we don't know exactly how many were living in United States territory. We do know that when the Europeans arrived, they brought many diseases that proved fatal to the Native Americans.

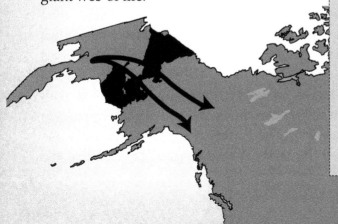

Imagine their surprise at how the colonists acted! The people who came to the New World wanted to create a new country with all of the comforts of the one they had just left. They didn't give any thought to their impact on the land or the people who already lived there. The colonists refused to accept that Native Americans had beliefs

We do know that when the Europeans arrived, they brought many diseases that proved fatal to the Native Americans.

and customs of their own. Colonists considered the natives to be heathens and savages—barely human at all.

And yet, the Native Americans were crucial to the colonists' survival. They taught the colonists how to use furs and pelts to ward off the winter cold, and how to prepare native crops. They even showed the settlers how to use snowshoes. Native Americans were guides for the colonists. They helped the colonists find their way in this foreign land. Foot trails the Native Americans had used for hundreds of years eventually became roads for the settlers as the colonies grew.

The colonists' arrival brought many changes to the lives of Native Americans. The colonists brought many diseases, such as smallpox. The native people didn't have any immunity to diseases brought from Europe because they had never been exposed to them. So while diseases such as smallpox sometimes killed the colonists, they almost always killed the native people. The result was that 80 percent of the Native American population was wiped out by European diseases.

Colonists brought guns, knives, and axes made of metal from Europe to the New World. These modern-looking items interested the Native Americans. They had used only primitive weapons before the settlers came. But access to modern tools changed the way the native peoples hunted and lived.

In many cases, the colonists and Native Americans got along with each other in spite of their differences. But some native people began to feel resentful of the newcomers. The Native Americans didn't like the impact the settlers had on the land. They damaged the land that the

Native Americans respected. Some colonists killed the native people, which caused the Native Americans to fight back. And, of course, if the native people attacked, there were plenty of colonists who attacked them back. Whether they were getting along or arguing, resentful or respectful, one thing is certain: the Native Americans influenced the early colonists tremendously.

Native American Trade

Once they were introduced to some of the colonists' modern tools and implements, Native Americans began to trade for these goods. They knew that they could trade animal pelts. This changed the reason why the native people hunted. Before the colonists arrived, Native Americans only hunted for their own needs: for food, pelts for blankets and clothing, and bones for tools.

After the colonists came, many Native Americans

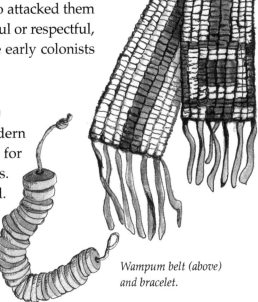

Wampum belt (above) and bracelet.

Make Your Own Wampum

1 Line the cookie sheet with aluminum foil.

2 Cut the Styrofoam into circles that are about 1 inch in diameter. An easy way to do this is to press a bottle cap into the Styrofoam to make a circular indentation as a guide.

3 Use the hole punch to make a hole in the center of each circle.

4 If you want to color your wampum, use permanent markers to color the surface of the Styrofoam discs. As you finish coloring each disc, set it on the cookie sheet. Make sure to leave space between each disc.

supplies
- cookie sheet
- aluminum foil
- Styrofoam trays
- scissors
- bottle cap
- hole punch
- permanent markers
- string

5 Now for the fun part! When Styrofoam is heated, it shrinks and becomes very hard. Warm your oven to a temperature of 225 degrees Fahrenheit. Place the cookie sheet with the discs on it into the oven for 3–4 minutes (if you have a window in your oven, it's fun to watch as they shrink). They will shrink to half their original size.

6 Carefully remove the cookie sheet from the oven. If any of your wampum pieces have curled up, you can use a spatula to flatten them.

Once they are cool, thread the wampum onto the string to make a bracelet or a necklace.

hunted with the intention of trading for items that they desired. In addition to animal pelts, Native Americans used "wampum" as a unit of trade. Wampum—short for *wampumpeag* or *wampumpeake*, an Algonquian word meaning a "string of white shell beads"—was the name European settlers gave to the beautiful strings of purple and white disc-shaped beads that were made by Native American peoples who lived near the sea. They used whelk (a type of ocean shellfish) shells to make the beads, drilling holes with a hand bow. Wampum shells were threaded onto string made from hemp or other plant fibers. Native Americans wore wampum around their neck and wrists, or as belts. Because it was beautiful and took lots of time to make, wampum was valuable. It was used kind of like money, and even tribes that lived far from the ocean had wampum. Wampum also indicated rank and dignity. Gifts of wampum showed great respect for the person receiving it.

Native Americans used "wampum" as a unit of trade.

Make Your Own Ball and Triangle Game

1 Break or cut the edges off the Styrofoam tray so that you have a flat piece to work with.

2 Draw a triangular shape on the Styrofoam—make each side of the triangle about 4–5 inches long.

3 Cut the triangle out of the Styrofoam and use scissors to make a 1-inch hole in the center of the triangle.

4 Punch a hole in one corner of the triangle and tie the string through the hole.

5 Roll a piece of aluminum foil into a ball small enough to fit through the hole in the triangle. Tightly tie the loose end of the string around the foil ball, and use half inch strips of duct tape to secure the string to the foil ball.

6 To play, grip the triangle by one corner opposite the string, allowing the ball to hang. Toss the ball into the air, then try to get it to go through the hole in the triangle.

supplies
- Styrofoam tray
- pen or pencil
- ruler
- scissors
- hole punch
- 18-inch length of string
- aluminum foil
- duct tape

Make Your Own Ring and Pin Game

1 Tie the string to the eraser end of the pencil.

2 Wrap tape over the knot to secure the string in place.

3 Tie the other end of the string to the plastic ring (if you don't have a milk jug ring, cut a ring shape from a plastic lid).

4 Holding the pencil point up, allow the ring to hang loose. Swing the ring up and try to catch it on the point of the pencil. See how many times in a row you can catch the ring!

supplies

- 15-inch length of string
- pencil with an eraser
- masking tape
- plastic ring from a milk jug (or a plastic lid)

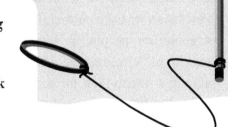

Native American Games and Toys

Native Americans played many games. The games varied by tribe, and many were based on physical skills. The point of many of the games was to help improve hunting skills. Foot races improved speed, hide-and-seek games were good practice for being silent, and archery games sharpened a hunter's aim. Are you surprised that Native Americans of long ago played the same types of games that you still play today?

Native American games used items found in nature or no equipment at all. With a little imagination, natural items could be turned into fun activities to occupy children and adults alike. Tree bark was used for a game called Ball and Triangle. Seeds acted as marbles. Nutshells were used as dice, and sticks or bones became musical instruments. One tradition that the Native Americans passed to colonists was the art of making cornhusk dolls. With materials that were readily available—and free!—children in the colonies could make baby dolls to play with.

Nearly every native tribe played a version of the game commonly called Ring and Pin. A target was fastened to a string, with a pin at the other end. The player tossed the target into the air and tried to spear it with the pin. The games differed

Corn husk doll.

Spotlight on Famous Colonists

Pocahontas

Pocahontas was a very important figure in the New World. An Indian princess, she was the daughter of Wahunsenacawh, more commonly called Powhatan (after the name of his tribe). Powhatan was the powerful chief of the Algonquian people in the Tidewater region of Virginia. Pocahontas probably saw white men for the first time around 1607. Captain John Smith was one of those men. As John Smith told the story, Native Americans took him captive and the great chief Powhatan welcomed him. Smith was then forced to stretch out on two flat stones while Indians held clubs menacingly over him. Then, a little girl—Pocahontas—rushed to his side, and pulled him to his feet. Though there are many stories about a romance between Smith and Pocahontas—probably started by Smith's own exaggerated account of their first meeting—they were really just very good friends. Historians believe that the scene John Smith described was a traditional "mock execution and salvation" ritual.

In July 1613, Pocahontas met a successful tobacco planter named John Rolfe. She began studying Rolfe's Christian religion, and was baptized and christened "Rebecca." The marriage between Pocahontas and John Rolfe in 1614 led to a general spirit of goodwill between the Native Americans and the English. In 1616, Pocahontas traveled to London with her husband, son Thomas, and a group of Algonquians to ask the king for more support for the Virginia Company. While she was in London, Pocahontas saw her old friend, Captain John Smith. On the voyage home to Virginia Pocahontas became ill and died. She was 22.

from tribe to tribe in the materials used to make this toy. Carved rings of bone, animal hide, dried squash, or even hair made into a loop acted as targets. The pin was made from cones, antler, or sometimes metal, if the tribe had contact with colonists.

Chapter 3

Life in a
Colonial Home

When the first weary settlers reached the New World after their long ocean voyage, they left their crowded, smelly ship behind in favor of solid ground. But the land they found was wild. There were no homes to provide protection from the elements. The colonists worked quickly to create some form of shelter. They made tents by cutting trees to make poles. They dug into hillsides to make pit houses. A handmade "cave" made three sides of a room. Colonists built sod houses by stacking squares of grassy turf they cut from the ground. The colonists didn't have access to any type of building materials, other than what nature offered, so that's what they used. These structures offered protection from harsh weather and wild animals, but they were far from beautiful.

Eventually the colonists replaced their temporary structures with permanent homes. Early homes in the

Early homes in the colonies were simple one-room structures.

colonies were simple one-room structures. Some houses were basic **wattle-and-daub** buildings, like those used for centuries in Europe. Others were made of lumber, either as whole logs built into a cabin or hand-cut boards. Some were made from local clay and mud bricks. These homes often had a dirt floor. This one room served many purposes—sleeping area, workspace, kitchen, and dining room. All of the people in a house fit into a space smaller than the size of our modern-day living rooms! There was little privacy.

Houses built later in the colonial period usually had several rooms. Sometimes they even had a second story. But even these homes were small by today's standards. In addition to a cooking area, the house might include a **parlor** and a hall, along with a staircase to an upper floor.

Houses had large, open fireplaces that were used for cooking, baking, and heating the home. Some of these fireplaces were large enough for the cook to walk into! Houses usually didn't have much furniture. Most colonists brought only a few things from the Old World, and furnished their houses with materials they gathered from the land.

Outbuildings provided space for tasks that didn't take place in the main house. The scullery was where people did dirty work such as laundry and soap making. Settlers used a springhouse to keep food items cool (remember, there were no refrigerators back then). And, of course, colonists used privies or "necessaries" as bathrooms. At night or in bad weather, people used chamber pots. They emptied their chamber pots into the necessary (or sometimes just tossed the contents out the window!).

A privy.

Privies

Colonial families didn't have indoor bathrooms like we do today. Outdoor bathroom facilities were called outhouses, privies, or necessaries. These were small outbuildings located away from the house. Inside, there was simply a board with a hole in it placed over a hole in the ground. Even if toilet paper had been available, it's unlikely that a colonial family would have spent their hard-earned money on such an extravagance. Instead, colonists made use of other materials: dried corn cobs, leaves, moss, or newspaper, if it was available.

These outdoor facilities were for day use, but if anyone needed to relieve themselves in the middle of the night, they used a chamber pot. In the morning, the chamber pot was emptied.

Colonial Homebuilding

One way English settlers built their houses was called wattle and daub. This method has been used for thousands of years by people like the ancient Greeks and some Native American tribes. Wattle and daub construction used simple materials that could easily be found in the New World—logs, thin branches, vines, clay, and sand. Colonists put upright posts—cut from logs—into the ground as the framework for their new homes. Then they wove thin branches, saplings, or vines between the upright posts to create the structure of the walls. Once this was complete, the settlers covered the structure with daub, which was a mixture of clay and straw. The colonists "painted" the daub with a limewash to protect the daub and to prevent it from deteriorating. The daub was an important part of the construction in cold climates, since it acted as insulation during the long New England winters.

Many colonial homes were made of brick. The materials needed for brickmaking were easy to find, and building a brick home, while hard work, was really pretty simple. Brick buildings were very common in Europe, and they probably made the colonists feel right at home. The thickness of the brick walls acted as insulation. They kept the cold weather out in the wintertime and kept the home cool during the summer months.

Because making bricks didn't require a lot of skill, it was usually a job assigned to indentured servants or slaves. Bricks were made from clay found on site. Brickmakers would fill a large area with clay, and then work water into the clay with their feet until the clay was a smooth consistency. They filled molds with the clay, then carried the bricks off to dry.

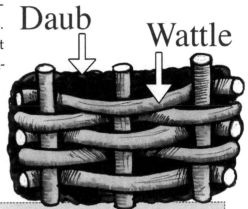

Daub **Wattle**

Dung Daub

Some colonists even mixed animal manure into their daub! The dung helped to prevent the clay from cracking. The dung-filled daub might smell a little stinky when the daub was fresh, but once it dried the smell was barely noticeable.

Colonial Words to Know

wattle and daub: a framework of woven branches and twigs covered and plastered with clay

parlor: a room used mostly for conversation and guests, kind of like today's living room—the word comes from the French parler, which means to speak

outbuilding: an extra building, separate from the main house

straw tick: a mattress or pillow filled with dried straw, leaves, grass, or cornhusks

Build Your Own Miniature Wattle-and-Daub House

1 Mark out a 16-inch square on the ground where you'd like to build your wattle-and-daub house. A sunny area is best.

2 At each corner and at 4-inch intervals along each side, dig a 6-inch-deep hole and set a straight stick into the ground. Tamp soil around each upright stick so that they are nice and solid.

3 Starting close to the ground, weave the thin branches in and out of the upright posts, leaving an opening for a door. As you weave, make sure you overlap the ends of the branches and that each layer you add is woven opposite the row below (if you weave around the front of a stick on the first layer, weave behind it on the next). At the door, wrap the flexible branches around the upright and back into the wall weave if possible, or trim off the excess with pruning shears.

4 To make the daub, put several handfuls of clay into the mixing tub and slowly start adding water. Use your hands to blend the water into the clay. If you come across any sticks or rocks, discard them. Keep adding water, a little at a time, until the clay is smooth and the texture of shaving cream.

5 Add some straw or dry weeds to the clay. Keep adding water if necessary to keep the texture right. The straw will help bind the daub together.

6 Using your hands, spread the daub over your house, completely covering the sticks and branches. You may need to do a couple of layers in order to completely cover the frame. If so, allow the first layer to dry before adding the second. Once all of the sticks are covered, smooth the surface out and allow to dry in the sun.

7 You can add a roof by laying strips of bark across the top of your house.

supplies

- 16 straight sticks, about 18 inches long and 1 inch in diameter
- small trowel
- hand-held pruning shears
- an armload of thin, flexible branches (willow works well)
- plastic tub for mixing
- clay soil and water
- straw or dry weeds
- strips of bark

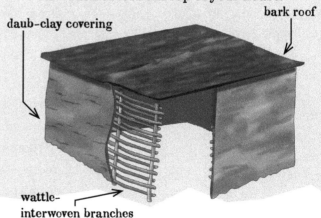

daub-clay covering

bark roof

wattle-interwoven branches

Build Your Own Bricks

You may not want to use your feet, but you can try your hand at creating some bricks of your own.

1 First, get the forms ready. You'll need your boxes to be completely open at what will be the top of your brick. In the case of soap boxes, you will have to tape the box closed, and then remove one large side of the box. Set your forms on a flat surface where you'll have room to work.

2 Now, make the mud. Put several handfuls of clay into the mixing tub and slowly start adding water. Use your hands (or your feet!) to blend the water into the clay. Add a handful of straw and blend that in well. If you come across any sticks or rocks, discard them. Keep adding water, a little at a time, until the clay is smooth and the texture of mashed potatoes.

3 Separate out a ball of clay that looks like it will fill your first form. Roll the clay in sand (to prevent it sticking to the form), then press

A Word About Clay

Clay soil isn't very good for growing plants, but it's great for making bricks. Explore your yard (with your parent's permission, of course) and see if you can find any clay. If the clay is dry, you might see a hard, cracked surface. If the clay is moist, it will feel a bit sticky and hold together when squeezed in your fist. What you don't want to use is any soil that looks like it would be good for a garden—loamy soil, with lots of organic material, won't stick together for brickmaking.

the ball into the form. Make sure you pack the brick down so that it fills the entire form.

4 Once all of your forms are filled, place them in an area that is sunny and warm. If you expect rain, remember to move them under a covered area—they need a chance to dry out completely. The drying process may take several weeks.

5 When you think your bricks are dry enough, carefully pull the cardboard away from the clay and then turn the forms upside down, pushing the brick out from the bottom.

6 You won't have enough bricks to build a house, but try stacking them into a little wall, just to see what it must have been like to use clay bricks as building material. You can use a really thin mixture of clay and water to help them stick together.

supplies

- ❧ small cardboard boxes—soap boxes or tea boxes will work well
- ❧ scissors
- ❧ tape
- ❧ clay soil
- ❧ plastic tub for mixing
- ❧ water
- ❧ straw or dry weeds
- ❧ sand

❧ The Colonial Bedroom ❧

The earliest colonists did not have bedding like we do today. They had to use bedding such as animal furs or a **straw tick**—with a log for a pillow! As colonial homes improved, the bedroom was more commonly known as the "best chamber." It was usually located on the first floor, just off the main living space, and was a place where important events such as births and deaths happened. Usually the kind of bed in the best room indicated the social status of the family: a grand bed belonging to the master of the house indicated high social status. Other members of the family shared beds; if visitors arrived they might even crowd into bed with the household members! Multiple beds in a room were common and bed partners might change nightly.

Sleep Tight!

The saying "sleep tight, don't let the bed bugs bite" refers to sleeping in a rope bedstead with a straw tick. Tight ropes on a bedstead meant a good night's sleep—as long as the straw tick wasn't harboring any bugs!

Make Your Own
Straw Tick

1 Collect the materials you'll use for stuffing during the middle of a dry day. If the stuffing feels damp at all, spread it out on newspapers to dry.

2 Once you're sure your materials are dry, stuff the pillowcase with them.

3 When you have it filled to your liking, you'll need to seal your straw tick. If you are comfortable using a needle and thread, use safety pins to hold the opening closed, then sew up the open end.

If you are using glue, run a line of glue along the inside edge of the mouth of the pillowcase. Use the clothespins to hold the edges together until the glue dries.

4 Once your straw tick is sealed, try it out—use it in place of your regular pillow for a night or two and see just how comfortable it is!

supplies

- ❧ dry grass clippings, leaves, cornhusks, or straw
- ❧ an old pillowcase
- ❧ needle and thread or glue
- ❧ safety pins or clothespins

Waste Not, Want Not

The colonists had a limited supply of materials. What couldn't be found in the New World had to be imported from Britain, making everything very expensive. The colonists didn't allow anything to go to waste—the corn harvest brought corn for meals, but the colonists had the sense to see that the cobs could be used for fuel and the husks for stuffing mattresses or crafting cornhusk dolls.

In the early 1700s, some beds had bed hangings, which were kind of like drapes, or curtains around the bed. These offered a bit of privacy in a room full of sleeping people. Bed hangings were also a sign of wealth.

Like most household items, early mattresses were made from natural materials that were readily available. Many colonists slept on straw ticks—a large fabric cover (kind of like a giant pillowcase) filled with straw, leaves, cornhusks, or grass. When the materials inside the tick became matted with use, colonists replaced the old straw with fresh filling. People had to make sure they used only dry material when they refilled their straw tick. If the straw was the least bit damp, the bedding would mildew, and the person would have to do the task over again. So if you were growing up in colonial times and your mom told you to "go make your bed," you would be doing more than just straightening the sheets and blankets!

Once the tick was filled, it was placed upon a rope bedstead. The bedsteads were made of wooden posts with holes drilled in them. The colonist would thread a rope in an out of the holes to create a grid of support for the straw tick. Over time, the ropes would stretch out, so they would have to be tightened.

Colonial Lighting

Colonial homes didn't have electricity, so people used candles for light after the sun set. The lady of the house was responsible for making candles. Candlemaking was hot and tiring work, but it was also a social time. Neighbors and friends usually gathered to help. Wealthier colonists might have a wooden candle mold to shape the melted wax, but most colonists used a dipping method.

Make Your Own Dipped Candles

This project will give you an idea of how time consuming candle-making was for the colonists. It's a project that requires adult supervision! Melted wax gets very hot and will burn you if you get any on your skin.

1 Fill a coffee can with cold water and set it near your work area.

2 Heat the griddle to 190–200 degrees Fahrenheit. Put the hard wax in the other coffee can and set the can onto the griddle. Carefully stir the wax until it is completely melted. This part will take a while—be patient! Keep the heat low and be safe. Use the hot pads if you ever need to touch the can. It will be hot.

3 Once the wax is completely melted, add the crayons. Now you're ready to start dipping.

4 Tie a metal nut or washer to each end of the wick for weight. Bend the wick in half over your finger—you'll be dipping two candles at a time. Dip the wicks into the wax for a few seconds, then lift them back out.

5 Allow excess wax to drip off, then dip the wick into the cold water. Continue the dipping and cooling process, making sure that the two wicks don't touch each other and stick together. Repeat the process until the candles have reached the desired thickness.

6 Trim the candle bottoms with a sharp knife so that they're flat.

7 Hang the candles to completely dry. Once they are dry, cut them apart and trim the wick to about one-half inch above the wax.

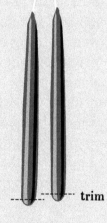

trim

supplies

- large coffee cans
- an electric griddle or frying pan
- plain paraffin wax (available at grocery stores or craft shops)
- an old spoon or wooden paint stirrer
- hot pads
- several old crayons, all the same color
- 20-inch length of wick (available in most craft and hobby stores)
- 2 metal nuts or washers
- knife

Safety tips

⚠ This activity requires adult supervision. The wax may not look hot, but it is!

⚠ Never leave hot wax unattended.

To prepare for dipping candles, women filled a large cauldron with tallow (a solid fat from butchered animals) or beeswax and heated it over an outdoor fire. Tallow was easy to come by and more common than beeswax for making candles. Colonists would tie a length of wick onto a stick, and dip the wick into the melted wax over and over. They would allow the wax to dry in between dips. The women dipped each candle until it reached the thickness they wanted. Then they cut the candle from the stick and stored it in a candle box. Candle boxes were conveniently placed in the home, either hung on a wall or set on a table.

Metal candlesticks held the candles on tabletops. Chambersticks were candle-

Make Your Own Candleholder

1 Glue the juice lid to the center of the CD, covering the hole.

2 Glue the film canister to the center of the juice lid, open side up.

3 Open the clothespin and put several drops of glue on the place where the clothespin comes together. Clamp the clothespin onto the CD and allow all of the glue to dry.

4 Use aluminum foil to completely cover your candleholder. Work carefully to make the tin foil as contoured to the candleholder as possible.

5 Place one of your homemade candles inside the foil-lined film canister. If it doesn't sit straight, drip a bit of wax into the holder, then quickly put the candle in place.

6 Now, with adult supervision, light the candle and see how carefully you must walk in order to keep the candle from blowing out. Never leave your candle burning unattended!

supplies

- an old CD
- metal juice lid
- all purpose or tacky glue
- film canister
- clothespin
- aluminum foil

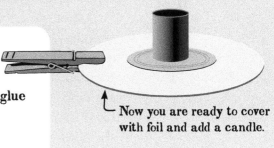

Now you are ready to cover with foil and add a candle.

Sometimes candles were used to tell time. Special candles made of uniform width were marked with equal bands. As the flame melted the wax, each melted band indicated that a certain amount of time had passed.

sticks with a small handle that colonists used to carry light with them to the bedchamber. Candle lanterns were a portable source of light that colonists could use outside. A small box of punched tin—or sometimes glass—protected the flame from wind and drafts.

A typical colonial family might have only 100 candles to use in a year's time. Because making candles was such hard work and so time consuming, the colonists tried to conserve them. That meant the colonists lived by the schedule of the sun—they began work when the sun rose and stopped for the day when it set.

Burning candles can drip hot wax, causing burns or fires. To prevent this, colonists used candleholders to take their candlelight safely with them. Colonial candleholders were most often made of tin.

✺ Picture This! ✺

Most colonial homes had very little decoration. Travelers to the New World could not bring much with them. Once the colonists got here, there weren't stores to shop in. Early colonial homes served the purpose of keeping colonists warm and dry—there wasn't much time for worrying about decorating. Of course, some household items could be both functional and pretty, such as window curtains, tablecloths, candleholders, and bedding. There wasn't even a family photo gallery, because cameras hadn't yet been invented. The colonists did have a couple of methods for capturing images, though, and these found their way to the walls of homes in the New World.

Just imagine that you are living an ocean away from your family and friends. Over the years, you have changed, and your family would love to have a look at you. Today, you would simply have someone take a photograph, and you could send it overseas—by mail, by fax, or, if you have a digital camera, by email. But in the seventeenth century people didn't have that luxury. If colonists wanted to create a likeness of someone, they had a few options, but they needed patience—all of them required the subject to sit still, so that their image or likeness could be captured.

Make Your Own Silhouette

For this activity, you'll need a friend to help out—either as a model or to create a silhouette of you.

1 Seat your subject about 12–18 inches away from a wall.

2 Shine a bright light onto your subject's head, so that their shadow falls on the wall. You may have to adjust the placement of the light and your subject—you'll want to make sure the shadow is sharp and details are clear.

3 Tape the black paper to the wall so that your subject's shadow is cast onto the paper.

4 Carefully trace the outline of the shadow with a pencil. Include as many details as you can—eyelashes or a curly lock of hair will make the silhouette more lifelike.

5 Once you're done tracing the shadow, take the black paper down and tell your subject to take a break. Use the scissors to carefully cut along the pencil line. Take your time!

6 Glue the detailed silhouette to the sheet of white paper.

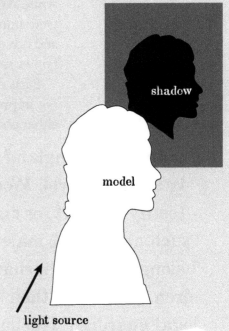

shadow

model

light source

supplies

- chair
- bright light (a desk lamp works well)
- black paper
- tape
- pencil
- scissors
- white paper
- glue stick

Of course, even today we must sit still for a photograph, but only for seconds. During colonial times, it took a bit longer.

One way to create a likeness was to have a portrait done. Professional artists created portraits on a canvas with oil paints, often over the course of many days. Portraits were beautiful and if the artist was good, the portrait looked a lot like the subject. But, because of the time and skill involved, they were also expensive. Many colonists couldn't afford such a luxury. Luckily, there was another option: silhouettes. Silhouettes captured a person's profile and could be done in a shorter amount of time by a family member. It required only a candle or lamp, black paper, scissors, and darkness.

❧ Keeping House ❧

Colonists came to the New World from many different countries, so the way they kept their homes varied widely. The Dutch, who settled in New Amsterdam, kept their homes spotless, surely a difficult task. They scoured their floors and walls, probably with sand, until they were white. Window glass—if any—was sparkling and fresh linen curtains were hung weekly. Of course, not every family kept their home so neat and tidy—visitors from other colonies found the cleanliness of the Dutch homes to be a bit odd.

Early colonial homes had dirt floors, but as the colonies grew and housing improved, many colonists built their homes with wooden floors. In either case, sweeping was necessary. Brooms were really the only way colonial housekeepers could clean their floors, since there was no such thing as electricity and vacuum cleaners! Colonists made brooms from flexible materials such as small twigs, broomcorn, or birch wood.

Puritan New England was most definitely a man's world! Women could not vote, testify in court, or sign legal documents such as wills. A married woman's wages belonged to her husband, and if any children were born, their father was the sole legal guardian. Husbands were even held responsible for their wife's behavior. If a woman committed a felony, her husband received the punishment!

A good broom probably took three nights' of time to make. A birch broom, for example, would start out as a 5-inch-thick log, approximately 6 feet long. The broommaker would remove the bark from the log and use a jackknife to carve one end into 14-inch-long slivers, leaving the slivers attached to the log. Then he would carve a second set of slivers the same length from the top section. The broommaker would bend down these top slivers over the shredded end and tie them together to make the bottom of the broom thicker. Then he would whittle the narrower end of the log into a handle, and trim the ends of the bottom slivers evenly. The broom would be ready to use.

Make Your Own Broom

1 To make the broom handle, open five sheets of newspaper all the way and stack them together. Roll the sheets together into a tight tube starting at the long edge. Secure with tape.

2 Fold three more sheets of newspaper in half, and in half again, following the fold lines in the newspaper. Measure down two inches from the last folded edge, and draw a line.

3 With scissors, cut from the edge opposite the line all the way up to the line. Do this with all three folded sheets of paper.

4 Lay one of the fringed sheets of paper on the ground. Set the broom handle so that one end is aligned with the folded (uncut) edge of the paper as shown. Wrap the fringed papers around the end of the broom handle so that the fringe hangs below the handle. Secure the folded edge to the handle with tape. Add the other fringed papers in the same manner.

5 Now, hold the broom by its handle and carefully fold the fringed ends so that they hang toward the floor. Push the rubber band down the handle and around the fringed paper to hold it in place.

←rolled paper for handle

cut to line to make fringe

roll and tape

secure with rubberband

supplies

- a stack of newspaper
- tape
- scissors
- a rubber band

In later colonial years some people had carpets in their homes, but it wasn't very common. Carpet was expensive to buy, so only the wealthiest families had it. Even then they were frugal about it—they bought a U-shaped "bed round" that fit around the bed, so that they didn't waste money on carpet underneath the bed.

Braided rag rugs were more common. Colonists made these rugs by braiding strips of scrap fabric, old clothing, or wool into long lengths. They then wound these lengths into a spiral and sewed them together to create flat rugs. The rugs provided a bit of warmth in the winter months.

Colonial rag rugs were used until they were completely worn out, and then they were thrown away. Because of this, there aren't very many examples of rag rugs today. We don't know for sure what size was common or how long it took colonists to complete a rug. We can assume that the rugs were made in a size that allowed people to easily take them outside for a good cleaning once in a while.

Wash Day

Colonial women had the chore of doing laundry, and it was a big job. The colonists used two tubs of water: one for washing and one for rinsing. Some colonists collected water in tubs during rainstorms; others hauled water from a nearby stream. Over a fire outside, they heated water and then poured it into tubs. Using large washing sticks, women churned the clothing around in the water until it was sufficiently clean. Then they moved the wet (and heavy!) laundry into a rinse tub. From here, they wrung each item out by hand and laid it out to dry on bushes or in grassy areas. White items were placed in direct sunlight, because the sun acted as natural bleach.

Easily soiled items like aprons, napkins, underwear, socks, and cloth diapers were washed most regularly. Outer clothing and bed linens were washed less frequently. During the winter months when drying clothing outside was impossible, the colonists washed their laundry indoors and dried it by the fire. Because this was difficult, they only washed the absolute necessities. The rest of the wash waited until springtime.

Make Your Own Braided Rug

1 First, you'll need to turn those T-shirts into usable material. Using scissors, cut them into strips 1–2 inches wide. To make this easier, you can tear the T-shirts: make a 2-inch snip at the bottom of the fabric, then place one hand on either side of the snip and pull. The shirt will tear easily. Your strips don't need to be perfect—once you're done, any imperfections will be invisible.

2 When you have a bunch of strips, tie many strips together, end to end, to make a length about 10 feet long. You'll be making a three-strand braid, so you will need three of these 10-foot-long pieces to work with.

3 To start braiding, gather three lengths of T-shirt "rope" and tie them together with a knot. Place the knotted end under the clipboard to hold it in place.

4 Now, you'll have to practice braiding three strands using only two hands! You will alternate crossing the left and right strands over the middle strand. The hardest part about braiding is remembering that the strands are always changing—once you cross a strand over the one in the middle, that strand then becomes the middle strand and will be crossed over next.

5 So, starting from the left, you'll move the left strand over the middle strand. Now, cross the right strand over the middle strand (which used to be the left strand). Back to the left side and cross it over the new middle strand. Once you get the hang of it, it's easy! See the diagram and if you need help, check with your mom or dad—odds are good that they can show you how to braid.

6 If you run out of material and still want to keep braiding, simply tie more T-shirt strips onto each strand. When you are done, tie the ends together in a knot to secure the braid.

7 To turn your braid into a rug, on a flat surface, start winding the braid into a coil. Use the needle and thread to secure the braid to itself as you go along. Keep turning the coil, sewing the braid in place until you reach the end.

length of braid created

supplies

- pile of old, worn out T-shirts
- scissors
- clipboard
- needle and thread

Anne Hutchinson

Ann Hutchinson was one of America's first feminists. She stood up for her rights at a time when few women did. Hutchinson was born in England, and she came to the colonies in 1634 with her husband and 15 children. She wanted to find a place that would allow people to worship in the manner that best suited their beliefs. She soon found that life in the Massachusetts Bay Colony, with its close ties between church and state, really didn't offer much religious freedom at all.

Hutchinson herself followed the Puritan religion, something she had in common with the Pilgrims who came on the *Mayflower*. But she didn't follow the religion exactly as other Puritans did. She had her own personal beliefs about faith and the almighty. The Puritans didn't like this—freedom of religion to them meant that other people could worship as they saw fit, but those of the Puritan faith must comply with the strictest interpretation of the Bible.

Anne knew that the Puritans did not support her opinions. She believed that faith was all anyone needed to go to Heaven, regardless whether or not they went to church. This idea didn't go over well with many people in the colonies. Anne organized a women's group to discuss matters of religion. She felt comfortable sharing her views with this group. Her opinions were interesting to the women, and each meeting found more people coming to hear Anne speak. Soon, men and women, along with magistrates and scholars, were attending her meetings.

The governor of the Massachusetts Bay Colony felt that Anne Hutchinson threatened the authority of the men in power. Wishing to silence her (after all, a thinking woman was a fearsome thing!), Governor Winthrop arrested her. As punishment, Anne Hutchinson and her family were banished from the community. They lived in exile on the island of Aquidneck, a small settlement in present-day Rhode Island.

In 1643, Native Americans massacred Anne and five of her children. Her critics saw this as God's final judgment for filling the heads of her followers with beliefs that did not exactly match the teachings of the Puritans.

Chapter 4

Colonial Clothes

Clothing was expensive in the colonies. People often had only one or two complete outfits, which they wore for years. Many people made their own clothing from **homespun cloth**, although people with money to spare bought their clothing and accessories from a **millinery shop**.

The millinery shop was a woman's business—the only business considered suitable for women in colonial days. *Milliner* means "hat-maker," but in addition to making hats, milliners offered hundreds of items for sale: fabric, needles, lace, jewelry, hosiery, and shoes imported directly from London. This meant that in the colonies the milliner's shop was the place to find the latest in fashion. Women could buy ready-made items, but some colonists shopped for lengths of fabric, thread, and other supplies for their own sewing projects.

Milliners also employed mantua makers. *Mantua* means "gown," and mantua makers were women who made dresses, jackets, and gowns for customers. They measured, cut, and draped the fabric to fit the customer and then did all of the sewing to create a finished product.

Sewing was done by hand, so even colonists who bought their clothing had "handmade" clothes. The cost of having clothing made by a local shopkeeper varied quite a bit, based on the detail, style, and quality of the clothing and the material used. Silk, wool, and cotton were some of the common types of material available.

All women wore a shift underneath their dresses. A shift was an ankle-length nightdress made from linen, with drawstrings at the neck and wrists. Women wore a shift both day and night, and most women had more than one. A woman would never wear only a shift, nor would she show her ankles or elbows: it was considered indecent.

On top of her shift, a working woman would wear a straight, ankle-length skirt with a lace-up vest called a bodice. Women often stitched bones (sometimes called stays) into their bodices to provide support and shape, but working women used very little boning, because it limited their movement and made working difficult and uncomfortable.

In the earliest colonies, aristocratic ladies—or those from the wealthy upper class—dressed a lot like working-class women. But not for long. For most of the colonial period, aristocrats showed their wealth through their clothing and felt that dressing as "commoners" was beneath them. These aristocratic ladies wore bodices with stays all the time, even while they slept. They often dressed in layers, though gown styles varied. Upper-class women wore petticoats under their gowns to make their skirts look wider.

During colonial times, cloth was very expensive. A dress that contained 18 yards of fabric was as valuable as a minivan is today! Because of this, dresses had to last as long as 15 years or more. Mending and updating by a tailor or milliner kept clothing in good condition for a long time.

Colonial Colors

Colonists used natural materials for dye to make different colors of cloth. Marigolds and goldenrod made yellow, cranberries made pink, walnut husks made deep brown, onion skins made golden brown, and blackberries made purple.

To make the colors "fast," or hold to the fibers, the dyes required a fixative. For this, colonists used alum and *sig*. You might have seen alum in your kitchen cupboard—it's used in cooking. But can you guess what *sig* is? It's stale human urine! Colonists worked *sig* into the fibers to make them colorfast.

Colonists are often depicted wearing black clothing (think of the Pilgrims), but in truth, black cloth was hard to come by. People lucky enough to have black clothing wore it only on very special occasions.

They also wore a cloth-covered basket frame on their hips called a panier that held their skirts out to the sides. A woman's wealth was shown in the type of fabric her clothing was made of—silk was an expensive luxury—and in special details, such as buttons and trims.

A colonial working man's clothing was simple. He usually wore a linen shirt and a pair of **breeches**. He also wore a close-fitting leather jacket called a doublet to protect his shirt from daily wear and tear. A gentleman wore a doublet as well, but his was less functional and more decorative. His doublet would have slashes in the leather to allow puffs of his undergarment to show. He also might wear a cape or a long coat over his tightly fitted breeches.

The colonists were careful with their resources; they patched and mended their clothing until the clothes were beyond repair. Worn out adult-sized shirts were cut down to make children's shirts. But even when it became impossible to mend clothing any further, colonists managed to find a way to use that material. For example, they turned worn out clothing and fabric scraps into rag rugs, which you read about in chapter 3.

Colonial Words to Know

homespun cloth: simple cloth made at home

millinery shop: a shop selling women's hats and clothing, as well as fabric, needles, thread, shoes, etc.

breeches: short trousers that go to just below the knee

flax: a plant with blue flowers whose long silky fibers can be spun into thread to make linen

✣ Making Clothing ✣

Many colonial families could not afford to buy clothing, or even to buy the cloth to make their own clothing. So they made their own cloth. To make cloth they had to start at the very beginning: they raised sheep for wool or grew **flax**, a fibrous plant that was used in textile making during colonial times.

Preparing wool or flax fibers for spinning was a job for the children. Turning wool into yarn for weaving and knitting was a tedious but very

Spotlight on Famous Colonists

Daniel Boone

One colonist who is famous for his unusual clothing style is Daniel Boone. Everyone knows he wore a coonskin cap, right? Well, actually, no. Daniel Boone wore a beaver hat, not the raccoon-skin hat with dangling tail that he's famous for. The coonskin cap myth came later, when an actor hired to play Daniel Boone in a minstrel show wore one, simply because he couldn't find a beaver hat.

In 1750, when Daniel Boone was 16, he moved with his family to North Carolina. Always a frontiersman and explorer, he spent time as a Conestoga wagon driver during one battle with Native Americans; many other battles followed. But it was when one of his acquaintances told him of a "secret door" through the mountains of what would become Kentucky that his famous pioneering began.

In 1773, along with his wife, Rebecca, their 10 children, and several other families, Boone set off in search of that mountain passage. In 1775, he founded Boonesboro, Kentucky, in spite of King George III insisting that none of his subjects settle beyond the Appalachian Mountains. Boone survived several years of Indian captivity during the Revolutionary War, and continued to move farther west. He died in Missouri at the age of 86.

important job. Children removed dung and debris from the wool. Then they "carded" it with special combs to make it ready for spinning. To prepare flax for spinning, children removed the seeds and crushed the stems. Then they removed the outer casing of the plant to reveal the part of the plant that would be turned into thread. Spinning with a drop spindle was a skill learned by most colonial children.

Wealthy colonists might import clothing from Britain, but shipping was often unreliable. Receiving an order could take months and months. No overnight delivery!

The spinning, dyeing, and weaving was typically done by the lady of the house, an older child, or by a servant. Spinning—or turning the fibers into thread—was an evening chore, because it didn't require much light. Once the wool or flax was spun into thread, it was dyed and then turned into sheets of fabric by weaving it on a loom. The colonists cut their clothing from this homespun cloth.

Knitting was another evening or rainy day task for colonial women. They used knitting needles to turn yarn of spun wool into commonly used items, most often stockings. Women sometimes knitted sweaters, but not as often. If they had fine thread, such as silk or cotton, and all of their other handwork was complete, women might knit lace for trimming clothing. Since lace trim was a luxury, this fancywork was pretty rare.

Just as children were expected to help with spinning, they were expected to learn how to knit. Children began knitting as young as 4 years old!

To weave string or yarn into flat cloth, colonists used large looms. A colonial loom was made of wood timbers and stood seven feet high. It took up as much floor space as a double bed! Because looms were so big, most common households didn't have them.

In New England, most people hired weavers to turn their spun yarn into sheets of cloth. Colonial weavers were considered a "cottage industry." This means that these

A woman spinning wool into yarn.

Make Your Own Yarn

1 First you'll make a drop spindle. Position the CD on the dowel, about 3 inches from one end. Wrap the dowel with electrical tape so that the CD fits snugly onto the dowel and will stay in place without sliding around.

2 Screw the cup hook into the end of the dowel farthest from the CD. The cup hook will be at the top of the drop spindle.

3 Tie the length of yarn onto the dowel, just above the CD. Pull the string through the cup hook and loop it around the hook once, to keep the yarn from slipping.

4 Use your fingers to pull apart a small amount of fleece until you have a fluffy handful of wool. Tuck the spindle under your arm, and place the end of the yarn over the prepared fleece. Hold the yarn and fleece firmly together with your left thumb and forefinger, dropping the spindle and allowing it to hang from the yarn.

5 Now, set the spindle in motion by pushing with your right thumb and pulling with your right forefinger (kind of like spinning a top). As the spindle turns clockwise, it will begin to grab the fleece, spinning it into yarn. Release more fleece as needed, by pulling with your right hand, all the while keeping the spindle turning.

6 When you have spun so much yarn that it's difficult to reach the spindle, unhook the yarn from the cup hook, wind the yarn you've spun around the dowel, and then rethread the spindle, making sure that the yarn is secured through the cup hook. Repeat steps 4 and 5.

7 Continue spinning until the spindle fills up with yarn, and then wind it into a skein or ball of yarn to be used in other projects.

This task definitely takes practice, but once you get the hang of it, you'll see how it's something that could have been accomplished in dim firelight. Can you imagine spinning enough wool, balls and balls and balls of it, to make an entire outfit?

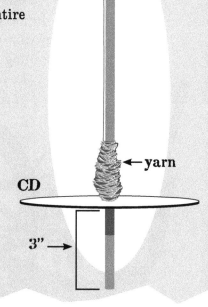

raw wool

← cup hook

← yarn

CD

3" →

supplies

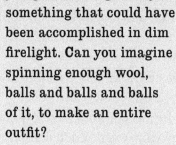

- an old **CD**
- ½-inch diameter wooden dowel, 12 inches long
- electrical tape
- small cup hook
- 2-foot length of wool yarn, purchased or hand spun
- fleece—available at yarn shops or craft stores

Make Your Own Marigold Dye

1 Measure the water into the pot and stir in the marigold petals. Allow to soak overnight.

2 With the help of an adult, heat the mixture on the stove and let it simmer for 15 minutes. Remove from heat and use the potato masher to crush the marigold petals. Return to heat and simmer for 15 minutes more.

3 Strain the mixture into a bowl, discarding the petals.

4 Now, roll your string or yarn into a coil and wrap the end around the coil once or twice to secure the string into a skein. This will prevent it from getting tangled.

5 Drop the skein into the pot of yellow dye and allow it to soak until the string reaches the desired color intensity. You may need to let it soak overnight for a really bright yellow.

6 Once your string reaches the desired hue, squeeze out the excess liquid and allow it to dry.

supplies

- 1 quart of water
- large pot
- 2 cups of marigold petals
- wooden spoon
- potato masher
- colander or sieve for straining
- about 10 yards of white cotton string (all-purpose kitchen string works well) or wool yarn spun in previous activity

weavers worked from their homes, or cottages, rather than at a shop in town. While spinning wool was generally a woman's job, weaving took a certain amount of strength and it was common for men to work as weavers. Some men were traveling weavers. They moved around the colonies, living with families in need of their services—it might take a professional weaver as long as a year to finish one family's weaving.

To begin making a length of fabric, the weaver strung a loom with "warp" threads that ran from the front to the back of the loom. These were strung tightly so that they were very taut. The loom had a special contraption that separated every other warp thread, making it easy for the weaver to push a tool called a shuttle between the threads. The shuttle was wound with "weft" threads that passed under every other warp thread. Then the weaver used foot pedals to reset the warp threads so

Make Your Own Finger Knitting

1 Tie a slipknot in the end of the string, leaving a tail about 6 inches long.

pull

2 Widen the slipknot enough that your thumb and forefinger can fit easily into the loop.

3 Reach through the loop, pinch the yarn and pull a new loop through. Be careful not to accidentally pull the tail of the yarn through the loop. Pull the new loop

until the original loop is snug—but not too tight—around it.

4 Reach through the *new* loop, pinch the yarn and pull another loop through. Continue pulling new loops through, each time pulling up the slack in the old loop. Continue this pattern until your chain is as long as you'd like.

pull

supplies

• a ball of yarn or string—if you have dyed your own in a previous activity, use that!

that the weft thread passed over and under the threads opposite those it passed through on its last trip. Each time the weaver pushed the shuttle between the warp threads, he or she used a beater bar (kind of like a giant comb) to push the woven strands of yarn tightly together.

A weaver could produce about six yards of cloth per day. The most common type of cloth was "linsey-woolsey," which was a combination of linen and wool yarn. The linen yarn was strung on the loom as the warp thread, and the wool yarn was wound onto the shuttle and used as the weft.

In the south, large plantations had plenty of room for a loom and slaves or indentured servants could produce cloth for the residents of the area.

A weaver at work on his loom.

Make Your Own Oatmeal Box Loom

Here's another way to try your hand at weaving—with this method, you'll end up with a circular tube of fabric that you can turn into a handbag or pocket.

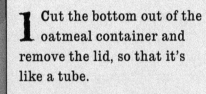

1 Cut the bottom out of the oatmeal container and remove the lid, so that it's like a tube.

2 Mark off notches at the top and bottom of the container, at ½-inch intervals. They should line up.

3 Use the scissors to snip a ¼-inch notch at each of these marks.

4 Tie a knot in one end of the yarn and tuck it into one of the notches. Now, string the yarn up and down, winding around the notches as shown, until you go all the way around the container. Secure the end of this thread into the last notch and cut. This will be your warp thread.

5 To begin weaving, cut a 5-foot length of yarn and tape one end to the craft stick. Push the craft stick in and out of the warp thread, pulling the yarn against the oatmeal container. Use the fork as

a beater and gently press the weft threads down to maintain a tight weave. When you run out of yarn, tie on a new length.

6 Keep working your way around the container until you reach the top.

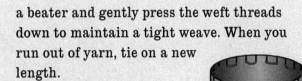

7 Tie off the loose end of the yarn, and then slide the weaving off of the container. Use the needle and thread to sew up one end, adding a finger-knitted yarn chain handle to turn your work into a handbag or a woven pocket.

supplies

- cardboard oatmeal container
- scissors
- ruler
- pencil
- yarn
- wooden craft stick
- masking tape
- fork
- needle and thread

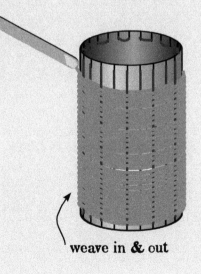

weave in & out

Make Your Own Cloth

1 To make your loom, remove the flaps from the cardboard box, leaving the top of the box open. **On the short sides of the box, use the ruler to mark ½-inch increments. Use scissors to make a ½-inch slit at each mark.**

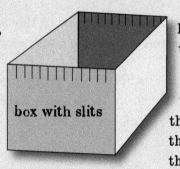

box with slits

2 Pick up the box loom so that you are holding the sides with the slits and set the box down in front of you. This puts the box in position for setting up the warp threads.

3 Starting at the left side of the box, push the warp thread into the left-hand slit nearest to you,

leaving a six inch tail. Tape the tail securely to the box.

4 Now, unroll the string and push it into the right-hand slit nearest to you. Wrap the roll of string under the box and through the next left-hand slit. Continue wrapping the string around the box, each time pushing the string into the next slit. Make sure you keep the string tight—but not too tight—as you wrap the box.

5 When you reach the last slit, cut the string and tape the tail to box.

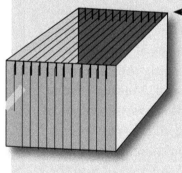

box wrapped with string

supplies

- ❧ sturdy cardboard box
- ❧ scissors
- ❧ ruler
- ❧ pencil
- ❧ string to be used for warp thread (white is fine)
- ❧ masking tape
- ❧ dyed string
- ❧ fork

❧ Colonial Accessories ❧

Accessories were an important part of colonial dress. Even the earliest settlers wanted to feel fashionable and wear things that made them feel special.

We think of pockets as being part of a pair of pants or a shirt, but during colonial times, pockets looked quite different. They were a separate piece of clothing. Ladies began wearing pockets during the late seventeenth century. Pockets were fairly large—perhaps the size of a

6 The string that you'll use for weaving is called the weft. To avoid getting tangled, work with lengths of string no longer than 10 feet.

7 Wind your weft string around a pencil, leaving a 12-inch tail. Starting from the right side of the loom, weave the pencil through the warp strings, over and under, until you reach the right side. Leave a 6-inch tail at the right.

8 Now you'll go back the other way, letting the weft string unroll from the pencil as needed. It's important to weave each row opposite the weave of the previous row. For instance, if you went *under* the warp thread at the end of the first row, you'll start the next row by going *over* the warp thread.

9 After you have woven three or four rows, you'll notice that the weft threads are a little loose. Traditional looms use a beater to press the fibers together, but for

this size loom, a fork will work. Every three or four rows, use the fork tines to gently press the weft threads together evenly across the row.

10 When you get to the end of your weft string, tie on another 10-foot length and wrap it around the pencil as you did at the beginning.

11 To remove your weaving from the box loom, turn the loom upside down and cut the warp threads. Tie pairs of warp threads next to each other together to close off your weaving. Trim off the loose ends.

top view

purse—and made of cloth. Women tied them around their waists, underneath their outer clothing. Colonists used their pockets to carry small items, just like we do today. Ladies would tuck things like spectacles, money, sewing implements, and keys into their pocket. For many women, their pocket was the only private space they had. Personal letters and other intimate objects tucked into a pocket were safe and private.

A pocket.

Make Your Own
Colonial-Style Pocket

1 Stack the felt squares with the edges aligned.

2 Use the plastic lid as a guide to round off the two bottom corners of the felt. Set the lid in each corner until it's touching both edges of the felt, then use the marker to draw a rounded line (see diagram).

3 Trim the corners with the scissors, making sure to cut through both layers of felt. Now, use the needle and thread to sew the pocket closed—starting at one of the top corners, sew down the side, across the bottom, and up the other side, stopping when you reach the top corner on that side. If you're not comfortable sewing, you can glue the felt together instead.

4 Use the hole punch to make two holes at the top of the pocket. Thread the ribbon into one hole and out the other. Tie the ends of the ribbon around your waist and fill your colonial pocket with some of your favorite belongings.

Sew 3 sides

Trim corners

supplies

- 2 felt squares, approximately 9 by 12 inches
- round plastic lid
- felt-tip marker
- scissors
- needle and thread or fabric glue
- hole punch
- 3-foot length of ribbon

In the colonial era, fashion started from the head down. Wigs for both men and women, a fashion that came from Britain, were popular as early as 1630. White wigs were considered a fashion accessory, much like earrings are today. Around 1770, tall, white wigs became fashionable for women in Europe, and they appeared in the colonies in the biggest cities, such as Philadelphia and Charleston (during colonial times called Charles Town after the king). Ladies who wore wigs were the cause of much comment because the

Lucy Locket

Have you ever heard the ditty about Lucy Locket? It goes like this:

Lucy Locket lost her pocket,

Kitty Fisher found it.

Not a bit of money in it,

Only 'broidery round it.

If you ever wondered how Lucy could manage to lose a pocket, now you know!

wigs were quite rare and made such a fashion statement. Those who wore these wigs rarely took them off, even at night. During the nighttime hours, some people actually set mouse traps in their wigs to prevent mice from nesting in them!

Men found that their wigs fit better on a hairless head, so they would pay someone to shave their head every two weeks. The finest wigs were made of human hair, although yak, goat, and horse mane were used as well. Wigs were covered with cinnamon and clove-scented animal fat and powdered with perfumed flour. Fine homes even provided a special powder room where guests could go to freshen up their wigs.

Hats were fashionable as well as practical. Fur and wool hats kept heads warm during cold winter months, while straw hats kept off the hot sun in the summertime. Hats also helped to keep ladies' hair clean in a dusty and smoky environment.

Gentlemen prided themselves on their hats, and seldom went anywhere without one. Even if a man wore a wig—making the wearing of a hat awkward—he carried his hat with him under his arm. Hats were made of felted wool or animal fur; some men's hats even had iron frames inside to protect the wearer from sword blows to the head.

During colonial times, it was considered improper for women to go about without a

Up until the age of six, young boys had long hair and wore dresses. At age six, boys were "breeched." They were removed from the gowns of childhood and their heads were shaved in preparation for their first wig. This custom initiated them into the world of adult men, and they were expected to act just as an adult man would.

head covering—leaving the house with a bare head was like going out only partially dressed! So most women and girls wore mobcaps, which were plain circles of material gathered around the head with a drawstring. The caps served a practical purpose, too. Covering up the hair prevented it from becoming soiled from all of the daily work. Dust and grease and smoke from cooking would all take a toll on hair. In a society where people didn't bathe very often (plus the colonists thought it was unhealthy to wash hair too often) it was easier to put on a clean cap.

Make Your Own Tricorn Hat

1 Cut the paper bag open so that the whole thing lies flat.

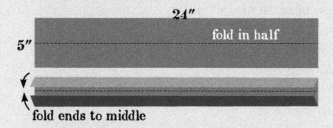

24"

fold in half

5"

fold ends to middle

2 Cut a 5-inch by 24-inch strip from one edge of the flattened bag.

3 To make the hat band, fold the strip of paper in half lengthwise, and then unfold it. Fold each long edge in to meet the crease; tape together. Roll the band into a circle with the taped edges inside, and fit it to your head, making sure that it isn't too tight. Staple or tape the band where the edges overlap.

4 Set the saucer and dinner plate onto the bag and trace around each. Cut the two circles out. Discard the rest of the brown bag.

5 To make the top of the hat, snip triangles about one-half inch into the smallest circle all the way around the edge to create tabs as shown.

supplies

- brown paper grocery sack
- scissors
- ruler
- pen or pencil
- clear cellophane tape
- stapler
- saucer (about $8\frac{1}{2}$ inches in diameter)
- dinner plate (about 11 inches in diameter)

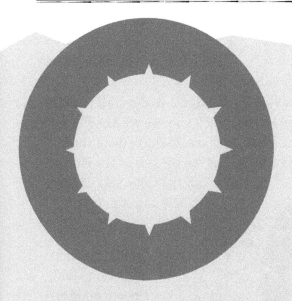

8 Fold the tabs on the top piece up. Set the hat band over this, so that the tabs are inside the band. Tape the tabs to the band.

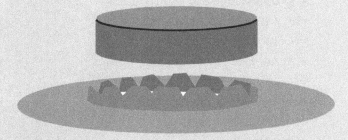

6 For the brim, fold the large circle in half. Measure and mark 3-inches in from the curved edge in 5 or 6 places. Connect these marks to create a complete arc, and then cut along that line, discarding the center piece. You'll be left with a doughnut shape. Snip triangles one-half inch in (similar to step 5) to create tabs in the inner circle.

9 Fold the tabs on the brim up, and then flip the brim so that it sits on the hat band with the notches inside. Tape the notches in place.

7 To put the hat together, remember that everyone has a different sized head! You may need to adjust the tabs a bit to make the pieces go together – either snip them a bit more, or fold them a bit less, so that the pieces fit together well. Be certain that the print from the bag is always on the inside of the hat as you are putting it together.

10 Turn the hat right side up, turn up three edges and tape in place to make a tri-cornered hat.

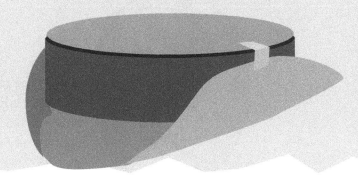

Make Your Own Mobcap

1 Cut an 18-inch circle from the fabric. (If there's a large round platter in your house, this might work as a template to trace around.)

2 Use a pencil to lightly mark a line 3 inches in from the cut edge, all the way around. Use your scissors to snip holes large enough to slip a safety pin through about 2 inches apart all along this line.

3 Pin a safety pin to the end of the ribbon.

4 Starting at any hole, push the safety pin up through one hole and down through the next one. To prevent the ribbon from accidentally pulling all the way through, use a bit of tape to secure the ribbon's end to the fabric.

gather material along ribbon

knot

Follow this up and down pattern all the way around the cap until you are within 2 inches of your starting place. Make certain that your last stitch leaves the tail of the ribbon on the same side of the fabric as your starting ribbon.

5 Lightly gather the fabric along the ribbon, making sure that the ribbon tails are of equal length. Tie a knot about 4 inches from the end of each ribbon to prevent the ribbon from accidentally being pulled out. If you'd like, you can glue or sew lace around the edge of your mobcap.

6 To wear your mobcap, place it on your head and pull the ribbon so it fits snugly on your head. Tie the ribbons in a bow to hold it in place.

supplies

- half a yard of cotton fabric or an old pillowcase
- pencil
- scissors
- safety pin
- 3-foot length of narrow ribbon
- tape
- lace (optional)
- glue/needle and thread

A mobcap.

Just as the caps kept one's hair clean, the opposite was true as well. Ladies who powdered, greased, and perfumed their hair—as was the style—slept with a mobcap in order to protect the bed linens from being stained by their cosmetics. Mobcaps were also worn under fancier bonnets and headpieces.

Wealthy men wore linen shirts trimmed with lace cuffs that extended beyond their jacket sleeves. These cuffs were white and very clean, making it clear to everyone that the wearer did not work with his hands. Wearing cuffs was kind of a status symbol, a way for men to show their wealth.

Wearing cuffs was kind of a status symbol, a way for men to show their wealth.

Fans in the colonial age were both fashionable and practical. They were useful for creating a breeze in warm weather, and they were also

In the seventeenth century, there were more than 500 fan manufacturers in Paris!

considered a necessary accessory to fashionable women's wardrobes. In proper dress, fans were as essential

Make Your Own Cuffs

6" tail   gather bubble wrap along ribbon   6" tail

1 Cut two pieces of bubble wrap 4 inches by 20 inches.

2 To make the first cuff, punch holes every half inch along one edge of the bubble wrap.

3 Tie the ribbon in place in one of the end holes, leaving a 6-inch tail. Lace the ribbon through the holes, coming up through one, down through the next, and so on, letting the bubble wrap gather along the ribbon as you go.

4 Fit the gathered cuff to your wrist and then tie the end of the ribbon into the last hole, securing it in place, again leaving a 6-inch tail.

5 Repeat with the second piece of bubble wrap.

6 To wear your cuffs, simply tie one onto each wrist.

supplies
- plastic bubble wrap (the kind used for packing fragile items)
- hole punch
- ribbon

Make Your Own Fan

1 Trace the template [here] onto tracing paper, and then tape the tracing paper onto the poster board.

2 Cut along the pencil line, making sure to go through both the tracing paper and the poster board.

3 Use the poster board piece that you cut out as a pattern, and trace nine more shapes onto the poster board. Cut these out.

paper fastener

4 Punch a hole in both ends of each piece, about half an inch from the end.

5 Use the markers to decorate each piece of poster board.

6 Stack the pieces and secure the narrow ends with the paper fastener.

7 Tie a bead to one end of the ribbon, so that it won't pull through the holes punched in your fan pieces. Thread the length of ribbon through the holes in the wide ends of the poster board pieces.

8 Fan out the pieces until the fan is all the way open and tie on a second bead to keep the fan from opening too far. Trim the end of the ribbon.

supplies

- tracing paper
- pencil
- tape
- poster board
- scissors
- hole punch
- markers
- paper fastener
- 2-foot length of ribbon
- 2 beads

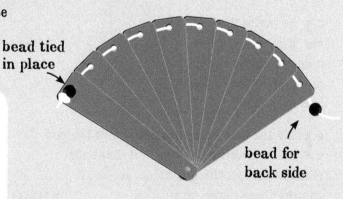

bead tied in place

bead for back side

Fan Talk

A fan could help a lady send subtle messages. During the eighteenth century, ladies were not supposed to speak their minds or openly show affection. Fans gave ladies a way around these rules of society. If a woman was angry, she could show it by striking the palm of the hand with a closed fan; if she felt jealous, she would flutter the open fan in front of her face; she could express concern by fanning quickly.

Fan language developed over the years, and the popularity of the fan continued into the nineteenth century with messages such as these:

Twirling the fan in the left hand—"We are watched"

Placing it on the left ear—"I wish to get rid of you"

Dropping the fan—"I belong to you"

Drawing across the eyes—"I am sorry"

Drawing the fan through the hand—"I hate you"

Resting the shut fan on the right eye—"When may I see you?"

Drawing the fan across the cheek—"I love you"

Covering the left ear with the open fan—"Do not betray our secret"

Resting the fan on the lips—"I don't trust you"

from Cool Breezes: Handheld Fans in 20th Century American Folk Art, Fashion and Advertising (Mid-America Arts Alliance)

as a pair of shoes. Fans also served other purposes, like flirting. A silent "fan language" evolved. Hidden behind a fan, young ladies could peek at activities that they really ought not see. Fans were used as masks, as memory aids for

In proper dress, fans were as essential as a pair of shoes.

Colonial Footwear

Colonists walked *a lot*. Their shoes were made of leather, in a style that they called "straight-lasted." This meant that shoes would work equally well on either foot, so they could be switched back and forth, creating a more even pattern of wear. Colonial shoes were most often closed with straps and buckles. Sometimes women closed their shoes with bows made from ribbon. Walking on muddy streets could quickly ruin shoes, so colonists wore special wooden clogs strapped over their shoes. The clogs were an inch or two high and prevented shoes from directly contacting the ground.

A colonist who needed shoes would visit a shoemaker. A shoemaker would have some ready-made shoes available for purchase, but if these didn't suit the customer, the shoemaker would custom-make a pair. The shoemaker would shape leather for the upper (or top part of the shoe) around a wooden form. Then he would sew the upper to the inner sole, then to the outer sole, or base, of the shoe. Finally, he would add a heel with wooden pegs. It took about 8 to 10 hours for a shoemaker to complete one pair of shoes.

parlor games, or even—when printed with slogans or pictures—as political propaganda. To manage a fan gracefully was considered an essential art for society women.

Beneath their clothes, plain or fancy, colonial Americans were likely to be a bit, well, smelly. Bathing in colonial America was a difficult task. Some people—those who knew how to swim, anyway—used streams and rivers to cool down and rinse off in the heat of summer. But many

Shoes would work equally well on either foot, so they could be switched back and forth.

Hand Sewn

People sewed in the colonial era without the help of a sewing machine, of course. The first sewing machine meant for use with cloth was invented in 1829 by French tailor Barthélemy Thimonnier. When Thimonnier installed 80 of his new machines in a clothing factory, tailors in Paris—apparently worried about losing their jobs to a machine—wrecked them! Early sewing machines were operated by hand crank or foot pedals, but didn't come into common use until the mid-1800s. The yards and yards of fabric used to make an elegant colonial gown were sewn together by hand, using just a needle and thread!

people found this practice to be a bit odd. When a colonist wanted to take a hot bath, he or she used a wooden tub. Colonists would haul the tub to an area where they would have as much privacy as possible, which usually wasn't much. He or she would then carry buckets of water from a well or nearby stream or pond, heat the water over a fire, and finally pour it into the tub. The process was so time consuming that colonists only bathed a couple of times a year.

Considering people's infrequent bathing habits, chamber pots dumped outside, and unrefrigerated food, just imagine the odors that might waft by the noses of colonial Americans! To combat unpleasant smells, colonists often carried pomanders. A pomander is a piece of fruit studded with cloves that

Washtub.

Even when there was a milliner available to colonists, sewing was an important skill for young girls to learn. Women took pride in their ability to make neat, even stitches and seldom went anywhere without a bit of needlework. Women took along mending, quilt patches in progress, or items such as curtains or tablecloths that needed hemming.

Make Your Own Pomander

1 Use a toothpick to prick small holes in the fruit where you'd like to have cloves—you can cover the entire piece of fruit in a random pattern, or create lines around the fruit.

2 Push a whole clove into each little hole, so the top of the clove sits on the fruit's surface.

3 When you have finished pushing cloves into the fruit, put the fruit into the zip-top bag with about a tablespoon of ground cinnamon; shake the bag to cover the fruit in cinnamon.

4 Tie a ribbon around the fruit and hang it in a cool, dry place for several weeks. Once the pomander is hard and dry, hang it in your room or, if you've made several, fill a bowl for a pretty, sweet-smelling arrangement.

supplies

- ☙ toothpick
- ☙ apple or orange
- ☙ whole cloves
- ☙ ground cinnamon
- ☙ gallon-sized zip-top bag
- ☙ ribbon

smells a bit spicy. Colonial women made pomanders that could be carried on outings or to help freshen the air in their homes. Pomanders were often used to help combat bad cooking odors in the kitchen.

Pretty Women

Women's cosmetics were made from items you might find in your kitchen today: flour, orrisroot (the root of an iris plant), and cornstarch. Ladies used these materials, as well as white lead (which we now know to be poisonous) to give their face the pale coloring that was fashionable. On top of this white base, they would add color to cheeks and lips, sometimes using color manufactured from crushed cochineal beetles. These insects live on prickly pear cactus and are still used in some cosmetics today!

Chapter 5

Colonial Farms and Gardens

There were no grocers or supermarkets during colonial times, so getting food to the table required a lot of work. Colonial meals were simple, but in order for families to have enough to eat, farming—from small kitchen gardens to giant plantations—was a critical part of colonial life. Almost all families in colonial America had at least small kitchen gardens with a few farm animals. Others lived and worked on large farms. Early colonists planted gardens to grow vegetables such as pumpkins, carrots, radishes, cabbages, and onions. Corn became a staple once the colonists learned its value from the Native Americans. In the Deep South, large plantations raised food crops as well as valuable **cash crops** such as **tobacco** and indigo.

Colonial Crops

Farmers who kept animals often grew hay. They harvested the hay, stored it in a dry place, and used it as animal feed during the cold winter months. It was critical that the hay be completely dry before being stored. If the hay was stored damp, it would start to rot or **decompose** (like a giant **compost pile**). The heat from the decomposition, trapped in the center of the pile, could cause the entire haystack to catch fire.

Apple trees came to the New World with the earliest colonists. Some brought small trees, others carried seeds to plant around their new homes. The climate in the northern colonies proved to be perfect for growing apples, and soon whole orchards thrived. Apples could be stored for up to six months, meaning that people had access to fresh fruit even during the winter. Apples were also turned into two colonial favorites: apple cider and applesauce.

Southern colonial plantations grew cash crops such as tobacco, indigo

Maize

The Native Americans introduced corn to the colonists with a different name: maize. The colonists happily added this grain to their gardens and their dinner tables, but they refused to use the Indian name for it. Instead, they used the term corn, which was a general name for any kind of grain.

The Native Americans used a method of planting that was quite different from the straight rows first planted by the colonists. Corn, squash, and beans, called "the three sisters," were the staple crops of many Native American tribes. Planted together in mounds, the corn grew tall and acted as stakes for the bean vines. The squash grew at the base of the corn, helping to keep the weeds down and the ground cool. The colonists soon imitated this Native American technique.

When the growing season ended, colonists harvested the corn and used it in a variety of ways. Fresh corn was eaten as **hominy** or roasted over the fire. Much of the corn harvest was dried, so that it would be available year round as a food source. Whole corn cobs were dried, then the kernels were removed from the cob. Children often did this chore as they sat around the evening fire, scraping the corn kernels off the dried cobs with the edge of a pan or shovel. The dry corn kernels were then ground into **meal**. Cornmeal was stored and used to make bread, Johnny Cakes (a kind of corn pancake), and porridge. The stripped corncobs were saved and used for kindling or for smoking meat. The colonists ate corn daily in many forms. They even made popcorn, sometimes eating it with sugar and cream for breakfast!

Make Your Own Apple Cider

1 Fold the cheesecloth so that it is 4–5 layers thick and use it to line the bowl. Make sure that there is at least 6 inches of cloth extending beyond the bowl, all the way around.

2 If you are using a food processor, set it up with the grating blade.

3 Wash the apples thoroughly. Quarter the apples (no need to peel or core) and grate them, either with the food processor or by hand. Dump the grated apple into the cheesecloth-lined bowl.

4 Pull up the sides of the cheesecloth and tie them securely together with the string.

5 Slide the bowl underneath a cupboard that has a strong handle, and tie the bag full of apple pulp so that it is suspended above the bowl. The weight of the apples in the hanging bag will push the apple juice through the cheesecloth and let it drip into the bowl.

6 When the juice stops dripping, you can squeeze the bag to make sure you get all of the juice out, then discard or compost the pulp. Enjoy a glass of fresh cider. Pour the rest into a pitcher and store it in the refrigerator.

supplies

- 2 yards of cheesecloth
- large bowl
- food processor or grater
- sharp knife
- a dozen apples
- string

Make Your Own Johnny Cakes

1 Beat egg in bowl. Stir in cornmeal, salt, and milk. The batter should be thick. You can add a bit more cornmeal or more milk to make your batter the right consistency.

2 Drop half cupfuls of batter onto a well-greased hot griddle and fry to a golden brown, a few minutes on each side. You may need to stir the batter left in the bowl occasionally to keep it well mixed.

3 Serve hot with butter and maple syrup or applesauce. Makes about a dozen.

supplies

- 1 egg
- 2 cups white or yellow cornmeal
- 1 teaspoon salt
- 1 to 1 cups milk
- bowl
- griddle
- butter

Make Your Own Applesauce

1 Peel the apples. Remove the apple core and slice the apples into the saucepan.

2 Pour the apple juice into the pan with the apples. Cover the pan and heat over medium-low heat for half an hour, stirring occasionally.

3 When the apples begin to feel very soft, use the potato masher to smash the cooked fruit into sauce (you can leave some chunks of apple if you like chunky sauce).

4 Stir in the cinnamon and serve, either hot or cold. Store leftover applesauce in the refrigerator.

supplies

- a dozen apples
- apple peeler
- sharp knife
- large saucepan
- 1 cup of apple juice
- wooden spoon
- potato masher
- 1 teaspoon cinnamon

Indigo plant.

(a plant grown to make a blue dye), and rice. Tobacco was a very labor-intensive crop. It grew best in soil that had not been used as farmland, which meant that each year new land had to be cleared for the next year's tobacco crop. Tobacco seeds were started in specially prepared seedbeds. When the plants reached a certain size, they were transplanted to the tobacco field. As the plants grew, plantation workers watched for the dreaded hornworm—a plague of these worms could destroy a crop in one week! If workers found these worms, they picked them off and

Colonial Words to Know

cash crop: a crop grown to sell for cash, like cotton or tobacco

tobacco: a plant that produces leaves that are smoked or chewed

decompose: to rot or disintegrate

compost pile: a pile of layers of plant debris, kitchen waste, and soil that decomposes into rich soil used to fertilize the land

hominy: part of the kernels of hulled corn either whole or ground

meal: the ground seeds of a cereal grass like oatmeal or cornmeal

perennial plant: a plant that comes back every year, compared to an annual, which dies at the end of the season

crushed them underfoot. Tobacco planters also had to trim the tops of each plant to encourage the growth of prime tobacco leaves.

Virginia soil grew the best grade of tobacco, where only the top few leaves were harvested. Elsewhere, production wasn't as high, and the entire plant was harvested. One farmer could manage only three to five acres per year, and every acre yielded about 5,000 plants. When the entire plant was harvested, each acre would yield about 500 pounds of tobacco. This was

Tobacco as Money

In the early days of tobacco farming, when tobacco was still scarce, the crop served as a sort of money for the colonists. Giving a specific value to tobacco is difficult today, because its value during colonial times was based on many factors. However, court records from Virginia give us an idea of tobacco's value in the late 1600s:

A day's labor: 20–30 pounds of tobacco

One-way trip across the Atlantic Ocean: 750 pounds

A bushel of beans: 40 pounds

A cow: 500 pounds

A horse: 1,500 pounds

A pound of sugar: 8 pounds

Spotlight on Famous Colonists

Eliza Lucas

As a newcomer to South Carolina, Eliza Lucas found herself running her family's plantation at age 17. Her father was a British army officer who spent time on the Caribbean island of Antigua. He moved his family to South Carolina hoping that the climate would be better for his sick wife. When Eliza's father was unexpectedly called back to Antigua, he left Eliza in charge of the plantation. She was also in charge of caring for her ailing mother. With seeds sent by her father, Eliza Lucas spent three years growing and processing indigo, experimenting with the processing until she perfected a method for creating hard cakes of indigo for dye. This dark-blue dye was used for coloring military uniforms and dress coats. The work of this young colonial woman created a very successful business for South Carolina farmers. By 1748, they had shipped 134,118 pounds of indigo cakes to England.

An infestation of tobacco cutworms (large, greyish caterpillars) or bright green hornworms could ruin crops. Colonial children were given the task of removing these caterpillars and crushing them between their fingers.

dried, bundled, and shipped to England in hogsheads (large barrels) that each held 1,000 to 1,500 pounds of tobacco.

Rice and indigo both grew well in the swampy conditions found in the Deep South. Unlike annual crops, which have to be replanted every year, indigo is a **perennial plant** that comes back every spring. But that didn't make it an easier crop to prepare for market. Indigo was harvested several times in a year. Farm workers would cut the stems and leaves of the mature plants and place them into large vats. They then crushed the cuttings and filled the vats with water. Left alone for a day, the mixture would start to rot. The stinky liquid was drained into a second vat and churned until sediment formed. You might think the sediment would be discarded, but that's actually what was kept. The sediment was moved to a third vat, where the moisture evaporated. The resulting paste was packed into wooden boxes and left to dry. This was an incredibly smelly process, and needed to happen at least a quarter of a mile away from homes so that people could avoid the stink. Flies were a problem, too, and young boys were assigned to spend the day fanning them away from the smelly vats.

Colonial Drinks

The colonists believed that drinking water could make them sick. They also didn't think milk was good for them. So what did people drink? Cider made from peaches or apples, or ale (a type of beer). It was common for both children and adults to drink ale, though it was watered down for colonial kids.

Colonial Companions

Some colonists kept animals as pets. Animals like cats and dogs arrived in the colonies by ship, just as their owners had. Cats helped to keep rats and mice at bay. Dogs were both pets and hunting animals. Wild animals such as deer and squirrels tamed by patient colonists made unusual pets. By around 1650, life settled down a bit in the colonies—the colonists had moved beyond the frenzied early years of day-to-day survival. They had built homes and planted gardens, and the New World was a familiar place so they managed to find a little time for pleasure. For some people, that meant capturing and keeping birds as entertainment.

Farm Animals and Game

In addition to raising vegetables and grains, colonists tried to put meat on the table. Hunting and fishing was one way to do this. Although there was lots of big game, like deer, colonists were often not very good at this type of hunting and busy with other tasks necessary for survival. They came to depend upon the hunting and fishing skills of Native Americans. Colonists would trade for their meat rather than hunting it. Clams, lobster, and other shellfish were also available to colonists living near the sea. With practice, colonists learned how to successfully put seafood on the table.

Livestock was imported to the colonies from Europe. Beef and pork became an important part of colonists' diets. The colonists didn't need to fence in their animals. They found that cows and pigs managed to deal with predators like wolves and panthers quite well on their own. When the settlers needed meat, they would round up one of their cows or pigs to be butchered. Farmers notched their animals' ears before they released them, so that they could identify them later. If a small farm had a milk cow or goat, she would be kept in a fenced area, so she could be milked regularly. Most milk was used to make cheese and butter, or in grain puddings. The colonists didn't think milk was very good to drink.

Mealtime Manners

When it was time to eat in a common colonial New England household, the men and older boys seated themselves at the table. The woman of the house would serve the meal, though she might sit next to her husband if there was an older daughter to do the serving. Younger children were expected to stand near the table behind the seated diners and eat what they were given in complete silence. If there was enough space, older children might sit once they completed their serving chores. Food was served in wooden trenchers, which were thick wooden plates. There was one trencher for every two people, who often used their fingers rather than utensils. Forks were quite uncommon, but people used spoons made of wood, bone, or pewter for foods that couldn't be eaten with fingers, such as soup. Napkins were linen (made from the flax plant) and quite large; clean ones were a necessity for each meal.

Colonial Cooks

People cooked their meals over an open fire. Sometimes they cooked outside, but more often they cooked over the fireplace in their home. The fireplace—or hearth—was used for cooking as well as heating the home. It was often quite large. Cast iron pots hung over the fire for cooking. Some homes had a swing arm that allowed the pot to be pulled out of the fire and closer to the cook. Cooking over an open fire with long skirts was very dangerous for women—the hem of their long skirts could easily catch fire, so they were always cautious.

Colonists often had beehive ovens that they used for baking. These ovens were giant domes of clay that were built outside of the home. Baking was done only once a week. On that day, colonial women baked enough bread to last the entire week. First, the cook would build a hot fire inside the oven to prepare it for baking. When the oven was hot enough, the cook raked the coals and ash out onto the ground. The clay retained enough heat to bake breads, cakes, and pies. Items requiring the highest temperatures were baked first, and as the oven cooled, items that baked at lower temperatures were added. There were no thermostats in those days; good bakers told the temperature of an oven to within a few degrees based on how long they could hold their arm inside the oven. Professional bakers could be identified by the lack of hair on their arms—it was singed off from all of that testing!

Without refrigeration, storing meat, milk, and cheese for long periods was difficult. The colonists stored foods that could spoil in a springhouse. Springhouses were the colonial version of a walk-in refrigerator. Water from an underground spring chilled the air. In some springhouses, the floor was a platform built over the water. In others, water flowed through a trough built into the dirt floor. Meat and fish were salted or smoked to preserve them, but fresh meat didn't last long. Pepper and other spices were in high demand as they helped conceal the taste of overripe meat.

Chapter **6**

Life and Work in a Colonial Town

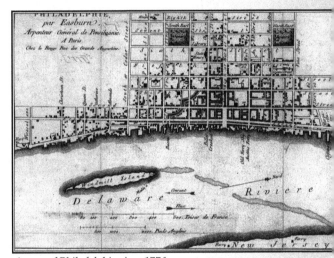

A map of Philadelphia circa 1776.

As more and more families arrived from Europe and settlements became successful, small villages began to emerge in the colonies. Many of those small villages became thriving towns. Places like Williamsburg and Philadelphia gradually transformed from one-horse towns into elegantly detailed colonial cities. Philadelphia's founder, William Penn, laid the city's streets out on a grid system. The streets that ran in one direction were numbered, and the streets that ran in the other direction were named after trees, such as Oak and Elm. Philadelphia is a good example of city planning.

Colonial Trades

As colonial towns grew, tradespeople set up shops offering their wares and services. Some of the tradespeople made products or did jobs necessary for survival in the colonies—blacksmiths made tools for clearing the land and farming, coopers crafted barrels for hauling water and to store food, and millers used giant windmills to grind grain. But people wanted non-essential

In Puritan New England, men of high social standing or wealth were called Master; their wives were called Mistress. Commoners such as shopkeepers or farmers were addressed as Goodman and his wife as Goodwife.

items, too. Eventually, colonists began to look beyond simple survival. People wanted to buy, rather than make, things like dresses, wigs, and baskets, so shops cropped up in successful colonial towns. Milliners, wigmakers, basketmakers, and apothecaries offered their wares to the townspeople and to those passing through.

Townspeople who knew the local craftspeople and their trades could easily make their way about town. But when newcomers arrived, they might not know where to find the services they needed. Shopkeepers wanted people to be able to find them, so they did what businesses do today: they hung signs. But there was one problem. Many colonists did not know how to read! Shopkeepers and tradespeople knew this, and did something very clever. Instead of simply using words on their signs, they included pictures that very clearly showed their services. A shoemaker's sign might show a picture of a boot. A hatter's sign would likely portray a hat. The sign for an apothecary shop might show a bottle or jar. Those images became familiar to the colonists, making it easy to find just the right shop or service.

Because of this demand, sign makers were some of the first artists in the New World. Colonial signs were painted and carved in wood and stone, formed in terra-cotta and plaster, painted on tiles, and made of metal.

Taverns were one of the first businesses to pop up in colonial villages and along well-used traveling routes. They offered tired and hungry travelers or newly arrived colonists a place to eat and a bed or floor to sleep on. Taverns were also one of the few public meeting places in the colonies. Townspeople gathered to discuss politics and business, or simply to visit.

Times Change

The colonial times covered a span of nearly 170 years. You can imagine how things changed from the time of the first settlement to the eventual formation of the United States of America. In the beginning, settlers arrived in a land that had no houses, no fields—not even familiar people to welcome them to their new home. Over time, though, small wooden homes peppered the colonies. Some colonists even owned mansions complete with finery such as paintings, detailed furniture, and silver. The owners of these fine homes were often wealthy men who came from England or colonists who had succeeded in creating a successful business in the New World.

Make Your Own Sign

1 Using the list of eighteenth-century trades (below), determine what type of sign you'd like to make. Think about what picture would make it clear to people the services that you offer.

2 On the paper, practice different designs until you are happy with the way your sign looks.

3 Sketch the design in pencil onto poster board.

4 Use paints to add color and detail.

supplies

- paper
- pencil
- 12-by-18-inch piece of cardboard or white poster board
- tempera paints

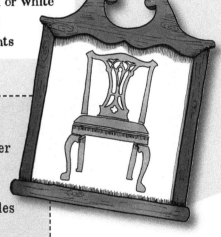

Eighteenth-Century Trades

Apothecary—pharmacist, doctor, dentist, and general storekeeper
Blacksmith—shaped iron into tools and horseshoes
Bookbinder—bound printed pages into books
Brass founder—made items out of brass like bells and shoe buckles
Brickmaker—crafted bricks from clay
Cabinetmaker—made furniture
Chandler—made candles
Cooper—made wooden barrels and tubs
Cutler—made and repaired knives
Farrier—put shoes on horses and sometimes acted as a veterinarian
Hatter—made hats
Miller—ground grain into flour
Milliner—made dresses and sold fashionable accessories
Printer—published the newspaper and often acted as postmaster
Saddler—crafted harnesses, saddles, and other leather items
Shoemaker—made and repaired shoes
Silversmith—made items like tea sets out of silver
Tavern keeper—provided meals, drinks, and lodging
Whitesmith—made items like candleholders and footwarmers out of tin
Wigmaker—made wigs

Make Your Own
String & Bead Puzzler

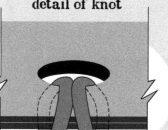

Puzzle your friends with this tricky challenge. It's easy to put together, but not so easy to solve!

1 Glue the two pieces of paperboard together, one on top of the other, to create a sturdy "board." Punch a hole at each end of the board.

2 At the center of the board, make a larger hole by punching overlapping holes. Make this hole big enough to accommodate four lengths of your string, but not big enough for the beads to pass through.

3 Fold the string in half, and push the looped end down through the center hole. Pull both ends of the string through the loop and pull

detail of knot

snug against the cardboard, making sure that the strings are not crossed (see diagram).

4 Thread one bead onto each length.

5 With the loop facing you, push each string end through the nearest hole in the board, and tie a knot in the end.

6 Now, try to move both beads onto the same loop of string without cutting or untying the string.

*Solution: see page 90.

supplies

- 2 pieces of paperboard, each 1 by 6 inches (a cereal box works well)
- all-purpose glue
- hole punch
- 18-inch heavy-duty string
- 2 wooden beads

Today's inns and taverns often offer television or reading materials to entertain guests. In colonial times, blacksmiths made tavern puzzles to amuse—and confuse—visitors. These puzzles were shown to curious folks with questions like "Can you remove the ring?" "Can you separate the pieces?" "Can you move this piece?" At a time when even books were scarce, puzzles and simple games such as these were counted on for entertainment.

Make Your Own
Liberty Bell Puzzler

← place on fold

Anybody can ring a bell. But can you UN-ring the Liberty Bell? This tricky tavern puzzle features the famous Liberty Bell and will surely stump your friends.

1 Cut the file folder in half at the crease.

2 Set the juice lid in the corner of one piece of the file folder and trace around it with the pencil. Put the saucer in the opposite corner and trace around it. When you cut these circles out, you'll have two different sized rounds.

3 Use the milk jug lid to trace a circle in the center of the juice lid–sized round, and the compact disc to trace a circle in the center of the saucer-sized round.

4 Snip a hole in the middle of the circle, and carefully remove the center circle from each, so that you end up with two rings.

5 Fold the remaining piece of file folder in half and draw the liberty bell using the template above as a guide. Cut this out, making sure that you don't cut through the fold. You'll end up with a double liberty bell.

6 Use the markers to color the pieces as you'd like.

7 Now to assemble the puzzle: double the big ring over, without making a visible crease.

8 Slide the small ring over one "leg" of the folded-over ring as far as it will go, then slip the liberty bell on, so that one of the bells slides into the space created by folding the big ring over. The bells will hang from the ring.

9 Slide the small ring down, so that it hangs over the liberty bell, and then open up the large frame. Now see if your friends can figure out how to remove the liberty bell without damaging the puzzle.

10 To solve the puzzle, simply do these steps in reverse.

supplies

- file folder
- lid from a can of frozen juice concentrate
- pencil
- scissors
- saucer (slightly larger than a CD)
- milk jug lid
- old CD
- red and blue markers

Busy taverns rented bed space, rather than whole beds. Overnight guests often slept head to toe in the same bed. Sometimes as many as six people shared a bed. Can you imagine spending the night in a bed with a bunch of strangers? Of course, guests were expected to remove their boots and spurs.

Colonial Craftspeople

As towns grew, so did the services they offered. Craftspeople who arrived in the New World were in high demand. Sometimes, colonial towns even advertised for the kinds of craftspeople they needed, so that their towns could expand and thrive.

Metalworkers

Metalworkers were skilled craftspeople who made many important goods for the colonists. Working metal was a tedious, time-consuming job. Metalworkers used hammers and other tools to pound, pinch, and twist hot metal into functional—and often beautiful—shapes. Each piece was made by hand, so no two items were ever exactly alike.

Brassfounders made items such as bells, shoe buckles, harness fittings, and furniture hardware. To make something out

The Liberty Bell

The Liberty Bell is considered a symbol of America's independence. It was made in London and arrived in Philadelphia in 1752. The bell weighs over 2,000 pounds and is 12 feet around. The original bell cracked during testing and was melted down and recast. The second bell was also defective. A third bell finally hung at Independence Hall, the state house for the colony of Pennsylvania and meeting place of the Continental Congress. The Liberty Bell sounded on July 8, 1775, to celebrate America's independence. It was rung on Independence Day every year until the bell cracked in 1835.

of brass, the founder would first make a three-dimensional model from soft metal or wood. A mold formed around these models made from a mixture of sand and clay would be able to withstand the 2,000-degree heat of molten brass. Molds were made in halves so that the founder could open it to release the model, leaving a hollow mold. Brass (usually scrap metal) was melted in a clay pot in a **forge**, or hot oven. When it was melted enough to pour, the founder used tongs to remove the pot from the forge and pour the liquid metal into the mold, through holes that had been carved for that purpose. This was hot and dangerous work! Once the metal

Make Your Own Tin Plate

1 Tear off a sheet of aluminum foil, big enough that it hangs over the edge of the plate by 3 or 4 inches.

2 Set the foil on the plate and, starting at the middle of the plate, very carefully use your hands to press the foil so that it conforms to the shape of the plate. If your plate has a raised edge, use your fingers (not fingernails!) to press the foil close to the plate—make sure that you don't allow any air space between the foil and the plate. When you reach the edge of your plate, neatly fold the edges of foil to the underside of the plate, and tape it down. **Press any rough edges smooth with the back of a spoon.**

3 Now, create a design. Use a toothpick to gently sketch a pattern

onto the foil. When you are happy with the design, press a bit harder with the toothpick to create an embossed pattern. You'll need to be careful not to tear the foil (you might want to dull the toothpick point before you use it by scratching it on a rough surface).

4 Use your new tin plate to serve fruit at your family's next meal.

supplies

- ❧ heavy-duty aluminum foil
- ❧ sturdy paper plate
- ❧ masking tape
- ❧ spoon
- ❧ toothpicks

cooled in the mold, the founder broke open the mold and took out the finished piece. Finally, he sanded and polished it. If the piece had working parts (such as harnesses or hinges), the founder checked to make sure the piece worked properly.

Blacksmiths made horseshoes, tools, hinges, latches, gates, and nails

Make Your Own Tin Lantern

1 First, make certain that the can doesn't have any sharp edges. If it does, use the hammer to tap the edge flat.

2 Use the marker to draw a design on the outside of the can. A simple design such as a star or sunburst is best.

3 Fill the can to within one inch of the top with water. Place it in the freezer overnight.

ice →

4 Meanwhile, find a flat surface where it's okay to do some hammering.

5 When the water in your can is frozen solid, lay several sheets of newspaper on your work surface. Roll more sheets of newspaper into two tubes and tape them onto the flat sheets of newspaper, about 2 or 3 inches apart, wide enough to fit your can in between.

6 Lay the frozen can between the newspaper tubes to prevent it from rolling around as you work.

7 Place the pointed end of the nail on one of the lines you've drawn on the can, and use the hammer to tap a hole in the can.

Punch holes along each of the lines in your pattern, leaving a space of one-quarter to one-half an inch between each hole. Always make certain that the area you are hammering is facing up, and you are hammering straight down, so that the nail doesn't slip down the side of the can.

8 If you need to take a break (after all, tinsmithing is hard work!), put the can back in the freezer until you're ready to work again. When you are finished punching holes, allow the ice to completely melt, pour the water out, and dry the can.

Melt some wax onto the bottom of the inside of the can and place the candle inside into the warm wax so the candle is not tippy or the tea light can't shift around. Remember, never leave a burning candle unattended!

supplies

- an empty tin can
- hammer
- a permanent marker
- water
- newspaper
- tape
- a 3-inch-long nail
- a candle or tea light

from iron. Whitesmiths—or tinsmiths—made lighter-weight items like candleholders, foot warmers, dippers, and strainers from sheets of tin imported from Britain or by reworking discarded items.

Silversmiths didn't appear in the colonies until close to the end of the seventeenth century and even then, only in larger, wealthier cities like Boston. The cost of silver was more than most colonists could afford. A silversmith made items such as tea sets, candlesticks, bowls, and pitchers. He made them by pouring molten (or melted) silver into a mold to form an ingot, or solid block, of silver. He then used a large hammer to pound the silver into a thick sheet. Hammering against an anvil (a large, flat block of iron), the smith pounded the silver into a thinner sheet of metal and slowly formed it into the desired shape. For an item such as a teapot, he would attach fancy handles with melted silver. Then he would polish the silver piece to a high shine.

Woodworkers

Nowadays, when we think of handheld tools, we're likely to list things like electric drills, electric saws, and electric screwdrivers. But in the seventeenth century, people didn't have electricity yet. So how did cabinetmakers and woodworkers cut wood or drill holes? By hand. Can you imagine ship builders making an entire wooden ship without the help of power tools?

A froe: tool for "slicing" off thin pieces of wood.

A colonial toolbox might include items with funny names such as log dog (used to secure a log in place while building a log cabin) and ring dog (a hook and ring used in pairs to carry or drag a log). Tools called augers made holes in wood in a variety of sizes. A small auger was called a gimlet. It was used mostly to make pilot holes for nails to be hammered into, since colonial nails often split wood if they were hammered in without a pilot hole. Drawknives and spokeshaves were used to shave wood into specific shapes, such as roof shingles or tool handles. Someone who worked as a cabinetmaker would have many woodworking tools, but the average colonist would have just basic tools. The metal parts of tools were formed by a metalsmith, but most colonists would make their own handles when they could.

One tool that you might find fun to use was called a pump drill, named for the pumping motion required to bore a hole. Colonists used pump drills to make holes for pegs in homebuilding or in other woodworking projects.

A hatchet.

Make Your Own Pump Drill

1 About half an inch from each end of one piece of cardboard, punch a hole. Find the center of the piece of cardboard and make a hole large enough that the dowel can slide freely through it. Try not to bend the cardboard as you do this. Use these holes as guides to make holes in the same places on the other two pieces of cardboard.

2 The pieces of cardboard will become the "push bar"—glue them together in a stack, making sure that the edges and holes line up. Put a large book on the stack so it stays flat and allow to dry overnight.

3 Hammer the nail part way into one end of the dowel. Use the wire cutters to cut the head off the nail. Then file the nail so that its tip has four sides that come together in a point. This will become the drill bit.

4 Screw the eyehook into the opposite end of the dowel.

supplies

- 3 pieces of sturdy corrugated cardboard, $2\frac{1}{2}$ by 10 inches
- hole punch
- $\frac{1}{2}$-inch diameter wooden dowel, 1 foot long
- all-purpose glue
- hammer
- nail
- wire cutters
- metal file
- small eyehook
- old compact disc
- electrical tape
- a cotton (not stretchy) shoelace, 40–43 inches long
- 2 beads large enough to fit on the shoelace
- old piece of wood

Colonial Words to Know

forge: a furnace or a shop with its furnace where metal is heated and wrought

bleeding: to remove or draw blood from—doctors bled patients for most medical ills during colonial times

apprentice: someone who learns a trade or art through the practical experience of working under someone skilled at that trade or art

apprenticeship: the period of time an apprentice serves to become skilled at a trade or art, usually several years

inoculate: to inject a vaccine

5 You'll need to mount the **CD** on the dowel 3 inches from the nail end. To do this, wrap enough electrical tape around the dowel that the **CD** fits snugly against the dowel. Glue the **CD** in place.

6 Slide the cardboard push bar onto the dowel above the **CD**. Tie a bead at one end of the shoelace and thread it up through one of the small holes in the push bar, through the eyehook and down through the hole in the opposite end of the push bar. Tie another bead below the second hole, so that the push bar stops about 1 inch above the **CD**.

7 Using a pump drill takes a little bit of practice, but once you have mastered the technique it's really easy (and fun!). Get a scrap piece of wood to practice on. Set the drill on the board, nail end down.

8 Holding onto the dowel, twist the push bar in a circle so that the shoelace winds around the dowel. When it's fully twisted, place your hands—one on each side of the dowel—on the push bar and gently push down. When the bar reaches the end of its slack, release pressure and allow the push bar to rise. The shoelace will wind around the dowel in the opposite direction (like a yo-yo), and you'll start the process over. All you need to do is keep the momentum going to drill a hole in the wood.

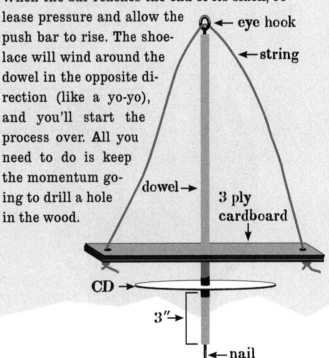

eye hook
string
dowel →
3 ply cardboard
CD →
3"→
←nail

✿ Colonial Medicine ✿

The colonists generally believed that nature provided a treatment for every ailment. Most of these treatments were herbal or from animals or metals, and were available from apothecaries. Doctor fees were high, and often colonists treated themselves. If a doctor came to help a patient, one favored treatment was **bleeding**. The doctor might use a variety of methods for this treatment, such as piercing a vein with a lancet, cutting the skin with a razor, or applying leeches. Unfortunately, this treatment often led to shock or death, due to loss of blood.

Just as any craftsperson, doctors were trained by **apprenticeship**.

Cotton Mather and the Smallpox Vaccine

Smallpox was a deadly illness that ravaged colonial towns and often ended in death. But smallpox, like chickenpox, was a disease that people could only catch one time. After that, the person was immune to the disease. Cotton Mather was born in Boston and educated at Harvard College. He had an intense interest in science, and learned of a folk practice for easing the smallpox problem from an African slave. Mather became convinced that smallpox could be prevented using this method. The fluid from a smallpox blister carries the smallpox virus. Mather believed that if a person was exposed to this fluid through an injection (similar to the shots you get at a doctor's office today), that person would contract only a very mild case of smallpox. The person would only get a little bit sick, and would also get a lifetime of immunity to the disease.

Many doctors didn't think this experiment would work. Some were quite angry that anyone would try it. But Cotton Mather convinced one other doctor, Dr. Zabiel Boylston of Boston, to give it a try. Dr. Boylston infected 300 Bostonians using Cotton Mather's experimental method, and the results proved that Mather was right. Two percent of the inoculated people died (6 out of 300), compared to 15 percent of the colonists who caught smallpox naturally (45 out of 300). Soon, this method of inoculation was used throughout the colonies and in Europe.

Bacteria were discovered in the late seventeenth century, but the connection between bacteria and illness wasn't made until after the colonial period ended.

But remember, there was no such thing as an X-ray, a blood test, or even an accurate diagram of internal organs during this time period. This made diagnosing medical problems difficult. The doctors who managed to learn more about the body than others did so illegally. They were often grave robbers who secretly dissected dead bodies!

🌿 Weather Watchers 🌿

Today, meteorologists predict the weather and share their forecasts on television, radio, and the Internet. They have satellites to help them see storms from high above the earth and radar to measure the strength of storms. During colonial times, predicting the weather was a bit more primitive.

Without modern technology, observing the weather was the most important part of forecasting. More than 350 years ago, the Reverend John Campanius Holm, a Swedish chaplain in the Swedes Fort Colony near what is now Wilmington, Delaware, recorded the first known observations about the weather. Other colonists kept detailed records of the weather as well. Benjamin Franklin is famous for kite flying in a thunderstorm, but in his job as a postmaster, he also tracked and kept records of a hurricane using a network of weather observers—other postmasters along the Atlantic Coast. George Washington and Thomas Jefferson also kept records of the daily weather.

Farmers and sailors were particularly interested in what to expect on the weather front. Crops could be ruined if seeds were planted too early or if rains came in the middle of harvesting. Sailors risked being caught at sea in wild—and often dangerous—weather.

In addition to watching the weather to predict storms or other weather events, colonists counted on weathervanes and barometers to help them predict what the weather would do. Weathervanes helped the colonists check from which direction the wind was blowing, and barometers helped them measure the air pressure. If the air pressure was high, it meant the weather would be nice. If the pressure was low or dropping, it meant bad weather was coming.

Travelers to the New World used weathervanes to gauge which way the wind was blowing. Based upon that, they could judge if a storm was blowing in soon, and if the weather was

Make Your Own Weathervane

1 Sketch a design on one 18-inch piece of cardboard. Animals, fish, and boats are common weathervane designs. When you are happy with your design, cut it out.

cardboard squares

2 Place the cutout shape on the second piece of 18-inch cardboard and trace around it. Cut out the second shape, following your traced lines.

3 Glue the dowel to one of your cardboard cutouts, placing it near the middle of the shape. Use a strip of tape to hold the dowel in place while the glue dries.

4 Cut two 2-inch squares of cardboard from your leftover scraps. Glue these alongside the dowel, one on each side.

5 Squeeze a dollop of glue onto each cardboard square and set the second cardboard cutout on top of this. Weight this down with a book and allow the glue to dry.

6 Once the glue is dry, use paint to decorate your shape.

7 To make directional arrows for the weathervane, cut an **X** shape from the third piece of cardboard, adding arrow points to each of the four ends. Mark the arrows with **N**, **S**, **E**, and **W** to indicate north, south, east, and west.

N
W   E
S

8 Cut a hole in the center of the **X** and glue it to the bottom of the small clay pot.

9 To try out your weathervane, find an area outside where the wind is unobstructed by buildings or trees. Stack the clay pots upside down on a flat surface. Position the directional arrows so that the **N** is pointing north. Slide the weathervane's dowel into the holes in the clay pots, making sure that the dowel will twirl freely.

10 Watch to see what direction the wind blows the weathervane.

supplies

- 2 pieces of corrugated cardboard, about 18 inches square
- pencil
- scissors
- 1/4-inch-diameter dowel, 18 inches long
- glue and tape
- paint
- 1 piece of corrugated cardboard, about 12 inches square
- 2 clay pots, each about 6 inches in diameter, with one slightly smaller than the other

good for traveling. Of course, weathervanes didn't tell the whole story; many ships were caught at sea in storms that were not predicted.

In the colonies, weathervanes helped farmers and sailors prepare for possible storms. In towns, weathervanes were mounted on tall buildings to catch the wind and be easily visible to the townspeople. In the countryside, people mounted weathervanes of their own.

Weathervanes were usually made of wood, copper, or iron and were often decorative, depicting animals such as whales, horses, or roosters. A home's weathervane showed a little bit of the homeowner's personality. Seaside homes were likely to display ships or sea creatures, while inland homes would be more inclined to feature wild or farm animals. One famous

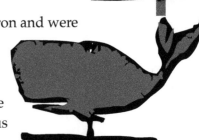

Make Your Own Barometer

1 Fill the bottle about three-quarters of the way up with water. Add several drops of food coloring and mix.

2 Insert the drinking straw partway into the bottle, making sure that the end of the straw is below the water level.

3 Seal the neck of the bottle around the straw with modeling clay, making certain that there are no gaps where air could escape.

4 Note where the water level in the straw is, then watch to see if it moves over time. You can also mark on the bottle where the water level in the straw is.

5 When the air pressure outside the bottle decreases, the trapped air inside the bottle will make the water in the straw rise. If you see this, watch for stormy weather. If the air pressure outside the bottle increases, it will push the water farther down in the straw, meaning fair weather ahead.

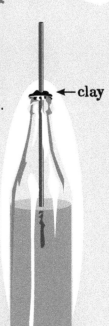

← clay

supplies

- clear glass soda bottle (don't use plastic—it's too flexible)
- water
- food coloring
- a clear, sturdy plastic drinking straw
- modeling clay

weathervane belonged to George Washington. To celebrate the end of the Revolutionary War, he mounted a weathervane in the shape of a peace dove on his home at Mount Vernon.

In 1643, an Italian named Evangelista Torrecelli invented the mercury barometer. With this new device, people were able to predict the weather more scientifically. Torrecelli's barometer was a bowl, half filled with mercury, and a test tube with its open end positioned under the surface of the mercury. As the atmospheric pressure changed, the level of the mercury in the inverted test tube rose and fell. If the pressure was high, the mercury was pushed farther down into the test tube. If the pressure was low, the mercury rose.

Torrecelli's invention led to the more common *"storm glass"* or "weather glass"—glass globes with a spout protruding from one side. Storm glasses likely came to the colonies with the first settlers, as they were standard instruments on ships. The rise and fall of the water in the spout offered a clue to coming changes in the weather. Water rising in the spout would indicate that a storm was 8–10 hours away, warning sailors to stay in port and farmers to hold off on harvesting crops.

A colonial-period barometer.

While mercury, which is poisonous, isn't a suitable material for you to use, you can use water to create a barometer of your own.

Crime and Punishment, Colonial Style

The colonists weren't perfect. There were robbers, murderers, and other lawbreakers, just like there are today. But some things that were considered criminal during the colonial period would make us laugh today.

The following description for how to find a witch comes from the days of the Salem Witch Trials: "With hands and feet tied, toss the suspected witch into a body of water. If she sinks, she is innocent. If she floats she is surely a witch." Which would you rather be—drowned or a witch?

For instance, meddling, or sticking your nose into someone else's business, was a crime. So was scolding, gossiping, falling asleep in church, and lying. In 1672, the Massachusetts General Court ordered that anyone accused of "scolding" (nagging or quarreling) should be either gagged (covering the mouth to prevent talking) or "set in a ducking stool and dipped over head and ears three times." The colonists

The Salem Witch Trials

No matter what their religious beliefs were, all colonists believed witchcraft to be the work of the devil and a sin. Witchcraft was blamed for many things the colonists didn't understand.

In January 1692, two young girls became ill. Their symptoms included seizures and screaming. This frightened the people of Salem, a town in the Massachusetts Bay Colony. A doctor was unable to come up with any other explanation, and said that the girls had been bewitched.

People were often afraid in New England in the seventeenth century. Illness was widespread, warring Native American tribes made colonists nervous and there was a strong belief in the devil. People easily believed the doctor's accusation of witchcraft. When the two girls "cried out" the names of the three women who had caused their pain, the women were arrested for practicing witchcraft.

These arrests were the first of many. Over the course of the year, more than 150 people were arrested for practicing witchcraft. All of these people were arrested only because some other colonists accused them of improper behavior. Of those arrested, 20 were found guilty and executed. Others died in their jail cells, but always insisted they were innocent.

Several months after the executions, a man named Thomas Brattle wrote a letter criticizing the witch trials. Thomas Brattle was a respected Boston merchant and Harvard graduate. His letter was convincing enough to make the governor look futher into the situation. In late November, Governor Phips ruled that people couldn't rely on evidence that couldn't be seen, heard, or felt. This meant that people couldn't tell the judge that they heard the devil's voice or saw a ghost as proof that someone was a witch. The remaining witchcraft cases were tried in 1693. This time, no one was convicted.

thought that public humiliation was the most effective form of punishment. Putting someone in prison was not a punishment that most people supported. It was considered cruel and a waste of taxpayers' money.

The colonists thought of themselves as moral and religious people, but they had a number of punishments in place to discourage people from acting inappropriately or breaking the law.

Criminal in a pillory.

The stocks were a wooden contraption that had holes near the bottom for the criminal's feet. With ankles locked in place, the criminal sat on a bench, which often had an uncomfortably sharp edge. The pillory was also made of wood, but had holes to lock a person's head and hands in place. The pillory—and the criminal being punished—was usually situated in the center of town. It was common for the public to jeer and throw rotten food—often fruit—at the criminal. A criminal sentenced to the pillory could hire someone to wipe his or her face to prevent suffocation. Sticky fruit caused another problem: it attracted insects, such as ants and wasps, making the criminal's time in the pillory even more uncomfortable.

Criminals were sometimes tied to a whipping post where they were whipped in front of the entire town or tied to the ducking stool, then dunked under water as many times as their sentence required.

Lawbreakers were sometimes given the option of paying a fine instead of enduring physical punishments. For instance, a thief might have to pay money along with so many pounds of tobacco, but the fine was usually much higher than the stolen goods were worth.

Colonists who committed a felony—a crime resulting in the loss of life or limb—risked death by hanging. But, because there was such a need for labor, the colonies didn't always enforce this type of punishment as strenuously as might have been done in England.

Fire bucket.

In some cases, criminals were branded at the base of the thumb on their right hand with a hot iron. This is where the custom came from of raising the right hand when being sworn in before a court or while taking an oath—this made it possible for the court to see a person's criminal record.

❧ Firefighters ❧

Fire was a worrisome problem in colonial America. Homes and buildings made of wood easily caught fire, especially because people used candles and lanterns for light and usually cooked with open fireplaces in their kitchens. In 1648, New Amsterdam (later New York City) governor Peter Stuyvesant appointed four men to act as fire wardens. Their job was to inspect chimneys to make sure that they were working properly.

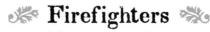

Later, eight men volunteered to form the Rattle Watch. These men patrolled the streets with fire rattles—wooden noisemakers—or muffin bells—made of small metal cups and a wooden handle. When a fire broke out, they would spin their noisemakers and instruct citizens to form a bucket brigade. A bucket brigade had two lines of people stretching from

Make Your Own Fire Rattle

1 Set the bottle caps top down on the scrap wood.

2 Use the hammer and nail to poke a hole in the center of each bottle cap. Make sure that the paper fasteners will fit through the hole you've made.

1½" 1"
12"

3 Starting 1 inch from the end of the cardboard, mark five dots, 1½ inches apart. Punch a hole at each mark.

4 To add the bottle cap rattles to the cardboard, push two bottle caps, tops together, onto a paper fastener. Push the paper faster through a hole in the cardboard and

put two more bottle caps on the end of the paper fastener.

5 Bend the ends of the paper fastener down to hold all in place, making sure to leave the caps loose enough to rattle and make noise.

6 Add the rest of the caps in the same manner. Practice rattling your fire rattle to make the most noise.

supplies

- 20 metal bottle caps
- piece of scrap wood
- hammer
- nail
- five, 1½-inch brass paper fasteners
- sturdy piece of corrugated cardboard, 2 by 12 inches
- hole punch

Save that Bed!

When a fire began to burn out of control, colonial firefighters opted to do the only thing they could: save valuable items. Two tools they used to save valuables were the salvage bag and the bed key. Firefighters used the salvage bag to collect anything valuable they could from inside a house. The bed was often the most valuable item in a colonial home. A bed key was a small metal tool that helped firefighters quickly take beds apart in order to move them out of the burning house.

The Rattle Watch was a group of men who patrolled the streets looking for fires. When they found one they would use their noise makers to alert citizens.

the town well or nearest water source to the burning structure. One line passed empty buckets hand-to-hand for water; the other sent buckets full of water toward the fire. Early on, buckets of water were tossed directly on the fire. Later, with the invention of the hand pumper, bucket brigades were used to keep the pumper full of water.

Because the bucket brigade was so important in putting out fires, every colonial home had a fire bucket. Owners of buildings that might be more likely to catch fire—a baker for instance—could be required to keep more than one bucket on hand. Fire buckets had their owners' name painted on them, so that after a busy firefighting session, people could identify their own buckets.

Solution to String & Bead Puzzler

pull loop

Let's assume that the front of the puzzle is the side where the loop is visible. Pull the loop down, so that the bead on the right can push through the central loop into the middle area. Now, pull on the two strings closest to the middle hole, until you pull the loop itself up through the hole. You'll see two new loops; pass the bead through these. Pull the two new loops back down through the center hole, then slide the bead through the original loop and onto the left loop.

Chapter 7

Colonial Communication

Today, if you were to move far away from your family and friends, you'd have many ways to stay in touch, like telephone, email, and instant messaging. But in the seventeenth and eighteenth centuries, the colonists really had only one reliable way to stay in contact with faraway friends and family—handwritten letters.

Colonial Letters

Paper was available in the colonies, but there wasn't much of it. Colonists made the most of the paper they had. When writing letters, people often filled every inch of a page. Colonists wrote with quill pens, which were cut from goose or turkey feathers and dipped in ink. Because quill pens often left puddles of ink, the letter writer would sprinkle sand on the paper to blot any excess ink. The sand was then poured back into its container and saved for the next letter-writing session.

Once a letter was complete, colonists didn't put it in an envelope like you would today.

Letters for the Postman

The way a letter was addressed in colonial America was quite different from the style used today. There were no street numbers, so the address was based on description. A colonial address might look like this:

To Mr. Faithfull Freeman, near the sign of the Plow, on Milk Street, Boston

Think about your house and nearby landmarks—how would you address a letter to yourself, using this method?

They carefully folded the letter so that all of the writing was concealed, then sealed it with wax and an insignia. An insignia was a symbol recognized as a person's special mark. Some people wore rings with their insignia on them—when sealing a letter, they'd just press their ring right into the warm wax. If someone broke a wax seal in order to read a letter that wasn't intended for them, it would be very difficult for them to hide what they'd done, because they wouldn't be able to re-seal it with the writer's seal. This guaranteed a certain amount of privacy

Mail could take months to get to its destination.

Make Your Own
Old-Fashioned Letter

1 Mix cornstarch, baking soda, and water in a saucepan. Cook over medium heat until the mixture forms a clay-like consistency. If you'd like, add a few drops of food coloring.

2 Dump the mixture onto a flat surface and allow it to cool a little. Knead until the clay is smooth.

3 Now you're ready to make your insignia. Roll a piece of clay into a short rope, about 1 inch in diameter.

4 Use the knife to cut a 2-inch-long section out of the rope, making sure that the ends are nice and flat (the shape should resemble a cork).

5 With a toothpick, carefully carve a design of your choice into one end of the formed clay. A simple design is better for this project. Allow the clay to dry on waxed paper overnight. (Wrap any leftover clay in a damp

supplies

- 1 cup cornstarch
- 2 cups baking soda
- $1\frac{1}{4}$ cup water
- food coloring (optional)
- butter knife
- toothpicks
- waxed paper
- a kitchen towel
- zip-top bag
- several sheets of paper
- ink pen
- wax candle, preferably dark colored
- vegetable oil

for letter writers. The blank side of the folded letter displayed the address of the recipient.

Early on, there was no postal service in the colonies, so letters were simply passed hand to hand as people traveled, until they reached their destination. Even when there was regular postal service, mail could take months to get to its destination.

The First Post Office

The first official notice of a postal system in the colonies came in 1639. The General Court of Massachusetts designated Richard Fairbanks's Boston tavern as the official drop-off place for mail brought from or being sent overseas. Later, a monthly post was set up between New York and Boston, and Pennsylvania's first post office opened in 1683. In 1737, Benjamin Franklin—who was 31 at the time—became postmaster of Philadelphia.

kitchen towel, store in a zip-top bag, and use to make marbles in a later project.)

6 Write a letter to a far-away relative. Imagine how surprised they will be to hear from you! Since you aren't using a quill pen, your letter will be easier to write than it would have been during colonial times.

7 When you are done, fold the letter as shown.

8 With adult supervision, light the candle and allow several drops of wax to form a puddle on a practice sheet of paper. Let the wax nearly dry, rub a little vegetable oil onto your insignia, then gently press it into the wax. It might take a bit of practice to know when the wax is exactly right for pressing the insignia into it. If the wax sticks to the clay insignia use a toothpick to clean it out.

9 When you've perfected your wax seal, drip a puddle of wax onto your completed letter where the folded sides overlap, and press in your insignia. Add a descriptive address that would help someone to find the recipient.

10 If you want to send your letter through the mail, you'll need to put it into an envelope and add a real address so that the postal service can deliver it—nowadays, street numbers and zip codes are required!

Cipher wheel.

❧ Colonial Codes ❧

When a colonist sent a letter containing private information, there was always the risk that a sneaky person would take a peek at it. After all, letters sealed with only a bit of wax and passed from hand to hand across the colonies might tempt a curious messenger.

During the mid-1700s, as the colonies geared up for the Revolutionary War, it was crucial for certain information to be kept secret.

Make Your Own Cipher Wheel

paper strips taped around lids

1 Use the hammer and nail to punch a hole in the center of each jar lid. Make sure that the hole you've made is big enough to slide onto the dowel. If the hole is too small, push the nail into each lid at an angle and turn it in circles to widen the hole a bit.

2 Use a pen or pencil to number the jar lids, from 1 to 20.

3 Wrap some tape around one end of the dowel to keep the lids from sliding off.

4 Make your cipher letters. Cut strips of paper wide enough and long enough to fit around the rims of your jar lids. The letters of the alphabet should run vertically and in random order down the strips.

5 Glue one strip around the edge of each jar lid.

6 To create a message, slide the jar lids onto the dowel, noting the order in which they are placed. Arrange one line of text to spell out your message.

7 On a piece of paper, copy down the line of letters just above your message. This is your secret code. To pass your message to a friend, you'll need to make sure that he or she has the same cipher wheel and two clues: the order in which the jar lids should be placed and the secret code.

8 To read a message, slide the jar lids onto the dowel in the proper order and arrange them so that the code letters line up. Now, look below the line of code for the message.

supplies

- ❧ 20 plastic jar lids—all the same size—such as those from mayonnaise jars
- ❧ large nail
- ❧ hammer
- ❧ ½-inch-diameter wooden dowel
- ❧ pen or pencil
- ❧ tape
- ❧ white paper
- ❧ ruler
- ❧ scissors
- ❧ glue

Make Your Own
Simple Paper Cipher

Here's another way to make a cipher similar to Jefferson's—but a bit easier.

1 Cut strips of paper long enough to fit around your cardboard tube, about ¼-inch wide. Write the letters of the alphabet vertically and in random order down the strips.

2 Now, wrap each strip around the tube and tape the end of each strip together. Depending upon the size of your tube, you may not have room for the entire strip; trim as necessary.

3 Create a message by rotating cipher strips to line up the letters you need. Choose any other line of lettering, and write those letters on a sheet of paper. This is your code.

4 Rearrange the paper strips to hide your message. To have a friend decipher the secret message, give him or her the paper cipher and the code. Putting the cipher strips in the proper order will reveal your message!

supplies

- paper
- scissors
- cardboard tube or container (such as a Pringles container)
- clear cellophane tape
- pen

Messages were passed between soldiers and generals in the colonies, as well as between America and Europe. European postmasters opened and read all mail, so it was difficult to keep anything secret. This problem inspired Thomas Jefferson to create a "cipher wheel" to pass secret communications after the Revolutionary War.

The cipher wheel was made from 26 wooden discs, each with the letters of the alphabet printed around the edge in a random order, threaded onto a rod. Messages were created

Thomas Jefferson

Thomas Jefferson

Thomas Jefferson was born in Virginia on April 13, 1743, nearly 150 years after the first colonists arrived in the New World. He studied at the College of William and Mary in Williamsburg, Virginia, practiced law, and served in the Virginia House of Burgesses.

When he was 26 years old, Jefferson inherited 5,000 acres of land in northern Virginia from his father. He began building a grand home he called Monticello. In 1772 he married Martha Wayles Skelton and brought her home to the partially completed mountain house.

In 1776, Thomas Jefferson—a member of the Continental Congress—wrote the Declaration of Independence. This document proclaims that all men are equal in rights, regardless of birth, wealth, or status, and that the government is the servant, not the master, of the people (interestingly, this did *not* mean freedom for slaves or equal rights for women). The Declaration of Independence was signed on July 4, 1776.

Jefferson served President George Washington as his secretary of state,

by rotating the discs to line up letters to form words. The message was visible on only one line, though other lines of random letters were also visible. Each of the discs was numbered. To reveal the message, the discs had to be assembled in the proper order. By writing down the proper order of the discs on the cipher wheel, along with a row of letters from one other line on the wheel (this was the code), the recipient of a secret message could decipher it using his own cipher wheel. The message recipient would assemble the discs in order, rotate them to display the coded letters, and then search the other lines of letters for the message.

and in this position made sure that people knew, understood, and followed the laws of the United States. During this time, he argued about politics with a man named Alexander Hamilton. Jefferson believed the government belonged to all of the people, but Hamilton wanted the rich to control the government. These differences led to the formation of the country's first political parties. People who preferred Jefferson's ideas became the Democrat-Republicans; Hamilton's followers became Federalists.

Thomas Jefferson became America's third president, serving from 1801 to 1809. Jefferson died on July 4, 1826, exactly 50 years after signing the Declaration of Independence.

While Jefferson made many political contributions to the young United States, he also created many inventions. In addition to the cipher, he designed a moldboard plow, which he used to turn his own soil. The moldboard sat directly on the ground, and when pulled by a horse, cut through the weeds and sod to open up the earth for cultivation. He also invented a spherical sundial that resembled a globe and used an elaborate system of lines to mark the passage of time.

A way that messages were passed in secret in the years leading up to, and during, the Revolutionary War, was with masks. You've probably worn a mask or two to disguise your face, but have you ever heard of using a mask to disguise a message? A clever person could write a letter phrased so that the recipient could use a special mask to reveal a secret message. The mask was a separate sheet of paper that, when placed over a page of writing, revealed the real message. The mask was sent separately from the letter, to make sure that the code couldn't be cracked while on its way to the correct recipient.

Make Your Own Secret Mask

1 First, decide upon the shape of your mask. Draw it on one sheet of paper and use the scissors to cut out the shape.

2 Now, lay your mask onto the second sheet of paper and very lightly trace the outline of the cut-out areas with the pencil.

supplies

- 2 sheets of paper
- pencil
- scissors

3 Write your letter on this sheet of paper, making certain that your secret message falls within the sketched area.

4 Creating a message within a message will take some clever thinking on your part. Once you've determined the secret message, you'll need to figure out how to hide these words within a longer letter.

Colonial Printers

Printing during the colonial period was all done by hand. The type for every document had to be hand set using tiny metal cubes with letters on them. These letters were arranged side by side in special trays in a print shop. The letters formed the words that made up a printed document.

The printing process required work by two men: a compositor and a pressman. The compositor set the type. This means he arranged the individual metal letters into words and sentences. The work was tedious and time consuming. The type had to be set backward, since printing reverses the image. Setting type for one page of a newspaper required 25 hours of hand labor!

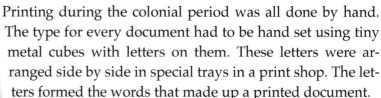

The Boston News-Letter

The *Boston News-Letter* was the first newspaper in America to be published on a regular schedule for an extended period of time. It made its first appearance on April 24, 1704. The Boston postmaster, John Campbell, founded the paper as a weekly and it continued as a weekly for over 70 years. In March 1776, the paper stopped publication when the American Revolution was in its early stages and the editor was forced to evacuate Boston.

Continental Congress

The first Continental Congress was a group of men who attended a meeting in 1774 in Philadelphia. Representatives from every colony except Georgia attended to discuss the relationship between the colonies and Britain. Their goals for the meeting were to record their colonial rights, identify Britain's violation of these rights, and decide how to get Britain to give them those rights. The members of the First Continental Congress agreed to boycott goods from Britain and to stop sending goods from the colonies to Britain, if Britain didn't cooperate.

The Second Continental Congress met in May 1775 and determined that Britain had declared war upon the colonies. In response, the Second Continental Congress established the Continental Army in June, with George Washington acting as commander in chief. Through the Continental Congress, the colonies acted as a joint force to stand up for their rights against Britain.

The pressman's job required a lot of strength. The pressman pulled a lever on the printing press to lower a pressure plate onto a sheet of paper. This plate pressed the paper against inked type under about 200 pounds of pressure. Each impression required 15 seconds of pressure, and then the paper was set aside to dry before the second side of the sheet could be printed.

Printers used their craft to create broadsheets, or flyers, and to print newspapers. Newspapers were usually printed weekly and were one of the few sources of information for colonists. With information taken from European newspapers, colonial newspapers offered news of happenings across the Atlantic as well as in the colonies. Newspapers and flyers also included letters and essays from readers, and advertisements for runaway slaves or items for sale. Most colonial newspapers were only four pages and measured 10 by 15 inches. The printer, who often acted as postmaster, often sold newspapers directly to the colonists.

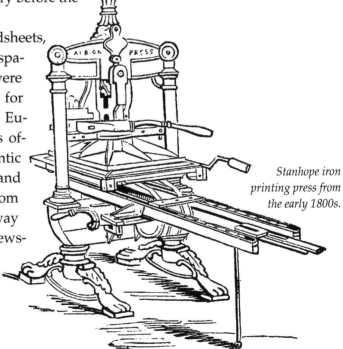

Stanhope iron printing press from the early 1800s.

Make Your Own Printing "Press"

1 Here's your chance to try writing backwards. On the bottom of the tray (the flat part), use the felt-tip pen to write a message. Remember, when you print, the letters and sentences will reverse. You'll need to start your sentence from the right side, rather than the left, and then use backwards letters to spell out your message. If you want to check it before you go any further, hold it up in front of a mirror—you should be able to read the message by looking at its reflection.

2 Now, use the pencil's dull point to press grooves deeply into the foam for each letter. You may need to go over the letter a couple of times to make a deep enough indentation.

3 Pour a small amount of paint onto the paper plate and dip the paintbrush into it. Dab most of the paint off onto the paper plate, so the brush isn't dripping.

4 Cover your entire message with paint, making certain that you don't use too much. If any of the grooved letters become filled with paint, use a toothpick to clean them out before you print.

5 Carefully set a blank sheet of paper onto the paint, and use the sides of your hands to press the paper onto the paint without moving the paper around.

6 Lift the paper off the Styrofoam tray and you'll see your message.

supplies

- Styrofoam deli tray
- felt-tip pen
- pencil with a dull point
- paint
- paper plate
- paint brush (or a foam brush from the hardware store)
- toothpicks
- paper

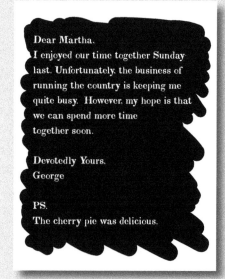

Dear Martha,

I enjoyed our time together Sunday last. Unfortunately, the business of running the country is keeping me quite busy. However, my hope is that we can spend more time together soon.

Devotedly Yours,
George

PS.
The cherry pie was delicious.

The Stamp Tax

In 1765, Britain passed what it called the **Stamp Act**, which was a kind of tax. This act required that colonists buy a special stamp and stick it to the paper items they used, such as newspapers, documents, or playing cards. Britain and **King George III** demanded that the money colonists spent on the stamps was sent back to England. The colonists were outraged. They didn't like being taxed by Britain, especially when they were not allowed to vote on such matters (hence the saying, "no taxation without representation"). Several British stamp agents (who had the job of making sure the colonists bought the stamps) were dipped in sticky tar and then rolled in feathers by angry colonists. King George III and Parliament took the hint—they repealed the **Stamp Tax**.

Bookbinding

Think about all of the places you can get books today: the public library, the school library, the store (if you have money). You can even find books  on the Internet with the click of a mouse! If you enjoy reading, you likely try out many new books each month, re-reading only your very favorites. Can you imagine having only a few books to choose from, your whole life?

Colonial bookbinder at work.

During colonial times, books were a luxury. They were mostly reserved for the middle and upper classes. Books were also status symbols. They represented wealth and education (remember, many people during colonial times could not read).

So, why were books expensive and hard to come by? All of the materials for books—paper for the pages and leather for the cover—were expensive and in short supply. Creating a book was a slow process. Books were put together by

Benjamin Franklin

Born in Boston in 1706, Benjamin Franklin was a writer, printer, inventor, and patriot. As a boy, he excelled in writing, but struggled with arithmetic. He was much more interested in inventing things than studying. One summer, he wanted to figure out how to move fast in the water. First, he tried paddles he made to specially fit his arms and help propel him through the water. He could go faster, but the paddles made his wrists and arms tired. He had more success with a kite—he floated on his back in the water and held onto a stick tied to the kite's string. The kite pulled him across the water! Ben Franklin was what we might call a "mover and a shaker."

When he was 12, Franklin's father apprenticed him to his older brother, James Franklin, who was a printer in Philadelphia. James had just come home from England with new printing equipment and was preparing to set up shop as a printer and publisher of the *New England Courant*. Benjamin signed a contract to work for James for 9 years in exchange for a room, food, training, and a small amount of pay. At 17, Ben took over printing of the *New England Courant*. His brother James had gotten into some political trouble and had to stop printing the paper himself.

Besides being a printer, Franklin was an asset to his community. He started a library system in the city of Philadelphia through a group he organized, called the Junto; he helped form the Union Fire Company and transformed the city's "night watch" (a group of volunteer citizens) into the Philadelphia Police Department with paid employees. In 1737, Franklin was named deputy postmaster of Philadelphia, and by 1753 he was the deputy postmaster general for all of the northern colonies.

In between all of that civic work, Franklin was writing. In 1733, under the name of Richard Saunders, Benjamin Franklin published *Poor Richard's Almanack*. Franklin's writing was both practical and comical and made

Poor Richard's Almanack the best-selling yearly journal in the colonies. The journal included lots of clever sayings—you may even recognize some of them:

- Early to bed and early to rise, makes a man healthy, wealthy and wise.
- Three may keep a secret, if two of them are dead.
- A penny saved is a penny earned.
- Diligence is the Mother of good luck.
- Fish and visitors smell in three days.

Benjamin Franklin was interested in electricity and experimented with it extensively. He set up a laboratory in his house after seeing an electrical demonstration by Dr. Archibald Spencer in 1746. He soon discovered that a mild electrical shock could kill a chicken. In a careless moment, he shocked himself badly and was able to determine that a shock strong enough to kill a turkey was strong enough to scare a scientist!

In 1752, Franklin conducted his famous kite-flying experiment to prove that lightning is an electrical spark. If he had known how risky some of his experiments were, he may have hesitated to put himself into so much danger.

Ben Franklin was a smart, sensible man and continued to become further involved in politics. The Pennsylvania Assembly elected him to represent the colonists in London. It was a chaotic time. King George III wished to continue to rule the colonies, but the colonists were tired of Britain's rules and taxes. Franklin stood up for the colonies against the Stamp Act and told the king that the colonists wished to be self-ruled. But England was in no mood to compromise.

Franklin headed home to Philadelphia as America headed toward revolution. In 1775, Ben Franklin was elected by the Pennsylvania Assembly as their delegate at the Second Continental Congress. The Continental Congress eventually voted for independence from Britain. Benjamin Franklin's signature at the bottom of the Declaration of Independence is a permanent reminder of his patriotism and belief in freedom.

Some of Benjamin Franklin's Inventions:

- Lightning rod
- Fireplace insert (or the Franklin stove)
- Bifocal glasses
- A chair that folded into a stepladder
- The harmonica (a musical instrument)
- Magic squares

Benjamin Franklin—unlike many of his colonial counterparts—took regular hot baths. He also took what he called a tonic bath. He wrote of them to a friend: "I rise almost every morning and sit in my chamber without any clothes whatsoever, half an hour or an hour, according to the season, either reading or writing."

hand at a place called a bindery. Book pages came from a printer. Bookbinders stacked the pages in order, then hand-stitched the pages together. Then the bookbinder folded the pages, trimmed them, and bound them with a leather cover. The cover was pretty, but more importantly, it protected the fragile paper inside. Often, the bookbinder would put decorative touches on the cover—tooled leather or letters embossed in gold leaf.

Colonial books may not have been plentiful, but they were treasures that would withstand repeated use and last for centuries.

bent rows

14	3	62	51	46	35	30	19
52	61	4	13	20	29	36	45
11	6	59	54	43	38	27	22
53	60	5	12	21	28	37	44
55	58	7	10	23	26	39	42
9	8	57	56	41	40	25	24
50	63	2	15	18	31	34	47
16	1	64	49	48	33	32	17

Magic Square

A magic square is a group of numbers arranged so that the sum of the numbers in each row, column, and diagonal is always the same. Ben Franklin's magic square shown here is eight numbers high and eight numbers wide, using numbers 1 to 64. The numbers in each row, column, and diagonal add up to 260. Half of each row or column adds up to half of 260. In addition, each of the "bent rows"—as Franklin called them—shown add up to 260.

Chapter 8

Colonial Kids

Colonial children lived a very different lifestyle than kids do today. In the colonies there was much work to be done and in each household, children were considered an important part of the work force. Children over the age of six were considered small adults. They dressed like adults and were expected to help with chores and work. Children rose early and often began the day by emptying the family chamber pot.

Adults usually passed the simplest (and often the most boring!) chores to younger members of the family. These were chores that needed to be done, but didn't take any particular skill. Husking corn, hauling wood, carding wool, and churning butter were just a few of the chores children helped with. Another was picking feathers from a live goose (yes, a live goose!). Kids did this three or four times per year. The feathers were used for making pillows and featherbeds.

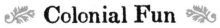 Colonial Fun

Once chores were done, colonial children—just like children of today— liked to play. Many of the games played today, such as hopscotch, hide-and-seek, tag, and leapfrog, were enjoyed by colonial children as well. Colonial kids played with toys that were much simpler than those you probably have today. While some stores sold children's toys imported from London, there weren't any toy factories in the colonies. Colonial toys were made from natural materials, such as wood, tin, and fiber, and there wasn't as great a variety of toys as there is today. Children who couldn't afford to buy toys made their own. They turned corn husks and rags into dolls, rolled barrel

Make Your Own Marbles

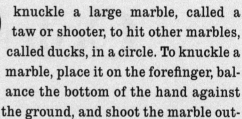

1 Mix cornstarch, baking soda, and water in a saucepan. Cook over medium heat until the mixture forms a clay-like consistency.

2 Dump the mixture onto a flat surface and allow it to cool a little before kneading. If you'd like, knead food coloring into it once it is cool enough to touch. You can try bright colors, or mix up some brown to make your marbles look more authentic.

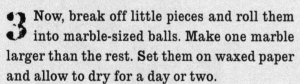

3 Now, break off little pieces and roll them into marble-sized balls. Make one marble larger than the rest. Set them on waxed paper and allow to dry for a day or two.

4 Wrap any leftover clay in a damp kitchen towel and store in a zip-top bag for another use.

There are many different variations of the game of shooting marbles. Players roll, throw, drop, or

knuckle a large marble, called a taw or shooter, to hit other marbles, called ducks, in a circle. To knuckle a marble, place it on the forefinger, balance the bottom of the hand against the ground, and shoot the marble outward with the thumb. To play marbles, lay out a large circle using a hoop (like a hula hoop) or a long piece of yarn or string. One marble game starts by placing a marble inside the circle. Then everyone gets a turn trying to hit the marble in the middle with a shooter. When a player hits the center marble he or she wins all of the marbles in the circle. In another game each player places a small marble in the circle. Everyone takes turns trying to knock or "shoot" marbles out of the circle with their shooter. Players get all of the marbles they shoot out of the circle.

supplies

- ❧ 1 cup cornstarch
- ❧ 2 cups baking soda
- ❧ 1¼ cups water
- ❧ food coloring (optional)
- ❧ waxed paper
- ❧ a kitchen towel
- ❧ zip-top bag

hoops, and spun tops that they made from a variety of materials.

One game that colonial children liked to play was marbles. People have been playing marble games for a long time. The oldest marbles ever found are over 4,000 years old! The ancient Romans had marbles made from stone and glass. But they didn't call their game marbles—they called it "nuts." Though the original rules to the Roman game are lost to us, playing with marbles is still popular. The term marble didn't come into use until 1694, when marble stone was used to make them. Colonial kids often used natural clay to make their marbles. You can use some common household ingredients to make your own.

Noise-making toys were just as popular in colonial times as they are today. The difference is that colonial toys didn't run on batteries.

A rag doll.

Make Your Own Whirligig

1 Set the plastic lid on the cardboard and trace around it. Cut the circle out of the cardboard.

2 Decorate the cardboard circle with a spiral or other geometric pattern. Make a mark at the center of the circle.

3 Punch two holes, one on each side of the center mark, about a quarter of an inch from the center of the circle.

4 Thread an end of the string through each hole and tie the ends together to form a big loop.

5 To play, center the circle of cardboard on the string loop and hold one end of the string loop in each hand. Making circular motions with your hands, twirl the circle until the string is taut. Now, pull your hands apart to set the whirligig in motion. You'll need to alternate pulling hard with relaxing to keep the whirligig spinning.

Twist disc until string is taught.

supplies

- a plastic lid, about 4 inches in diameter
- a piece of stiff cardboard
- markers or crayons
- scissors
- a hole punch
- 2½ feet of string

Make Your Own Apple Doll

1 Using the vegetable peeler, remove the skin from the apple.

2 Push a pencil firmly into the blossom end of the apple; this will help you to hold the apple steady as you carve the face.

3 Using the knife or toothpicks, carve a face in the apple. Carve eyes and a mouth about one-fourth of an inch deep—if they are too shallow, they won't be visible once the apple shrivels up.

4 Put the entire apple into the zip-top bag with a couple of tablespoons of lemon juice. Seal the bag and roll the apple around until it's covered with the lemon juice. Then take the apple out and dry it off with a paper towel.

5 Fill the bottle partway with sand or gravel to weight it down and stick your carved apple head (still attached to the pencil) into the sand. Don't let the apple rest on the edge of the bottle. Air needs to circulate around the whole apple to prevent mildewing so add more sand if necessary. Keep it in a dry place until the apple is thoroughly shriveled—this may take several weeks, depending on the weather.

6 Once the apple is dried, dump the sand or gravel out of the bottle. Now make sure the apple head sits securely in the bottle, then glue all around the rim of the bottle and press the dried apple into the glue. Allow to dry.

7 Glue a bead into each eye socket. You can collect and tape on dried sticks for arms, if you like. To dress the doll, drape fabric scraps around the bottle until you're happy with how it looks, then glue them in place. Add extra touches like yarn for hair, a hat, lace collar, or other colonial finery and your apple doll will be complete.

supplies

- apple
- vegetable peeler
- pencil
- plastic picnic knife
- toothpicks
- lemon juice
- zip-top bag
- paper towel
- empty dish soap bottle
- sand or gravel
- tacky glue
- beads for eyes
- dried sticks
- masking tape
- fabric scraps
- lace, ribbon, yarn, or other decorations

Parents made toys for their children from items like wood, cloth, paper, or leather. Whistles and rattles are two types of noisy toys that a colonial child might have played with. Another was called a whirligig. Made from coins, wood chips, or buttons, whirligigs make a buzzing noise once you get them spinning.

Children in colonial times played with dolls, too. But, just as with most toys, their dolls were made of materials that were readily available. With a little imagination—and maybe some scrap fabric—pine cones and sticks could become baby dolls. The Native Americans taught the colonists to make cornhusk dolls, and rags made lovely rag dolls. Colonists even turned apples into apple dolls by peeling a raw apple, carving a face into it, and letting it dry. Each apple face dried differently, so no two faces were ever alike. The dried apple heads mounted to a body made of sticks and dressed in scrap fabric became cherished toys.

Colonial Education

Colonial boys received an education, because it was important for them to at least know how to read and do math well enough to prevent being cheated. Colonial girls often weren't so lucky. In areas where a school was available, boy students far outnumbered girls, although some girls did attend school where they learned to read and cipher (solve math problems). Generally a girl's education focused more on household duties such as cooking, needlework, spinning, and knitting. Girls usually learned any book-knowledge at home, practicing their letters and numbers on cross-stitched samplers or compiling a receipt (recipe) book. For some boys, education was part of their apprenticeship at a trade.

In *Child Life in Colonial Days*, Alice Morse Earle recounts one colonial farmer's objections to girls attending school. "In winter it's too far for girls to walk; in summer they ought to stay at home to help in the kitchen." Now isn't that silly?

But even when schools were available, many children did not attend because they were too busy helping at home. In colonial times, children were a necessary part of the workforce and only had the luxury of education when all of the chores were complete.

Some colonial schools were "dame schools," where a lady taught lessons from her own home. In other cases, schools were one-room buildings where students sat on long benches. The dictionary—one of the few

Make Your Own Hornbook

1 Measure and cut out a 10-inch-by-6-inch rectangle of cardboard from the cereal box. Save the rest for later. Trim the cardboard into a paddle shape by removing a 2-by-2 inch square from each of the top corners.

2 With a hole punch, make a hole for hanging your hornbook in the narrow end, and tie the string through the hole to make a loop.

3 On the paper, neatly write out the alphabet, using both uppercase and lowercase letters. In the remaining space write a favorite phrase—either one of your own, or one from Ben Franklin list on page 103. Make sure you leave at least a half-inch border at each edge of the paper.

4 Cut the page protector to 6-by-8 inches. Set a single layer of the trimmed page protector over the piece of paper.

5 From the cereal box, cut two 6-inch-long strips

and two 8-inch long strips, each half an inch wide. Carefully cover the strips with aluminum foil, making the surface as smooth as possible. Punch a hole in both ends of every strip, a half inch from the end.

6 Set the foil-covered strips around the edges of the plastic page protector, and punch holes to match through the page protector, paper, and cardboard. Now use paper fasteners to hold all of the layers together. If the paper fasteners extend beyond the edge of the cardboard, simply snip them off with scissors.

supplies

- cardboard cereal box
- ruler
- scissors
- hole punch
- string
- 6-by-8-inch piece of paper
- pencil or pen
- plastic sheet protector
- aluminum foil
- paper fasteners

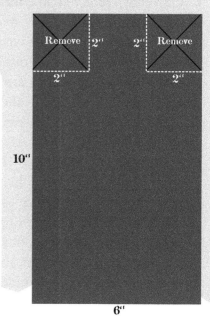

Remove 2"   2" Remove
      2"   2"

10"

6"

How Did They Do That?

To get the layer of horn used to protect the paper on each hornbook, a cow or ox horn was soaked for several weeks in water. This separated the bony core from the horn. With the core removed, a lengthwise slit was cut in the horn, which was then heated and flattened. A horn is made of many layers, and this process caused the thin, transparent layers to separate and peel away.

real books in most schools—was a treasured resource and placed on a table of its own.

The schoolmaster at a one-room schoolhouse was often a young man who had just graduated from college. He had a seat at the front of the school. The schoolmaster usually didn't get paid very much, maybe only a bible and a place to stay.

Colonial schools didn't have textbooks as we know them. Paper in the colonies was scarce, so students turned to birch bark—plentiful in the eastern forests—as a substitute. Each student wrote out arithmetic rules on the bark and then bound the bark into a kind of book.

Children learned to read from hornbooks. These were not really books at all, but small, wooden paddles with printed letters of the alphabet, common syllables, and a prayer or proverb mounted on them.

During the wintertime, some schools required children to bring a stick of wood for the fire each day. Any student who forgot that essential contribution sat in the seat farthest from the warmth of the fire as punishment.

Covering the sheet of printed paper was a thin protective layer of cow or ox horn (that's why they were called hornbooks). This way children could learn to read, even though books and paper were often hard to come by, and hornbooks could be used year after year.

Harvard College

Harvard College was founded in 1636 in Cambridge, Massachusetts, for training Puritan ministers, though other young men attended the college as well. All instruction was offered in Latin.

Glossary

A

anvil: A heavy steel or iron block on which blacksmiths hammered metal into shapes.

apothecary: Pharmacist, doctor, dentist, and general storekeeper.

apprentice: Someone who works for a tradesman for a designated period of time while he learns a specific skill.

apprenticeship: The period of time an apprentice serves to become skilled at a trade or art, usually several years.

ascend: To rise from a lower rank; when a new king or queen has begun ruling.

B

blacksmith: Someone who shaped iron into tools and horseshoes.

blasphemy: A disrespectful attitude or language about God, religion, or something sacred.

bleeding: To remove or draw blood from—doctors bled patients for most medical ills during colonial times.

bookbinder: Someone who bound printed pages into books.

brass founder: Someone who made items out of brass like bells and shoe buckles.

breeches: Short trousers that go to just below the knee.

breeching: The removal of a young boy from the gowns of childhood.

brickmaker: Someone who crafted bricks from clay for use in building.

C

cabinetmaker: Someone who made furniture.

cash crop: A crop grown to sell for cash, like cotton or tobacco.

chamber pot: A container used indoors as a bathroom facility.

chandler: Someone who made candles.

charter: Permission from the king, allowing a group to settle a portion of land and govern it as the group sees fit.

chattel: Any property, movable or immovable, except real estate. Women in colonial times were considered chattel.

cloak: A long, protective outer garment usually made of a heavy woolen fabric.

cobbler: A craftsman who mends or makes boots and shoes.

colonize: To establish a colony.

colony: A settlement in a foreign place.

compost pile: A pile of layers of plant debris, kitchen waste, and soil that decomposes into rich soil used to fertilize the land.

cooper: Someone who made wooden barrels and tubs.

cordage: Rope.

craftsman: A skilled worker.

cutler: Someone who made and repaired knives.

D

decompose: To rot or disintegrate.

dung: Animal feces or droppings.

E

earthenware: Dishes and pots made of baked clay.

F

farrier: Someone who put shoes on horses and sometimes acted as a veterinarian.

flagon: A container with a handle used to serve liquids.

flax: A plant with blue flowers whose long silky fibers can be spun into thread to make linen.

forge: A furnace or a shop with its furnace where metal is heated and wrought.

fortnight: A period of two weeks.

freedom dues: Compensation given to indentured servants upon their release.

G
game: Wild animals, birds, or fish hunted for food.

green: A grassy area usually located at the center of a town and set aside for common use. Also called a common.

H
hammock: A swinging netting or canvas supported by cords from supports at each end.

hatter: Someone who made hats.

hogshead: A large wooden barrel used to transport tobacco.

homespun cloth: Simple cloth made at home.

hominy: Part of the kernels of hulled corn either whole or ground.

hornbook: A wooden paddle with a piece of paper showing the alphabet and a verse, used in school lessons.

I
indigo: A plant that yields a blue dye.

inoculate: To inject a vaccine.

L
loft: A low space or attic directly under a roof.

M
magistrate: A public official authorized to judge dilemmas bought before a court of justice.

maize: Native American word for corn.

mason: One who builds or works with stone or brick.

meal: The ground seeds of a cereal grass like oatmeal or cornmeal.

miller: Someone who ground grain into flour.

milliner: Someone who made dresses and sold fashionable accessories.

millinery shop: A shop selling women's hats and clothing, as well as fabric, needles, thread, shoes, etc.

mobcap: A common hat with a puffed crown and a floppy brim made of ruffles or lace.

mutiny: A revolt against those in charge.

N
Navigation Acts: Rules that governed what could be shipped in and out of the colonies and by whom.

necessary: An outdoor bathroom facility, also called a privy.

New World: The continents of North and South America.

O
outbuilding: An extra building, separate from the main house.

overseer: A person in charge.

P
pacifism: The belief that all conflict can be resolved peacefully.

pallet: A straw mattress or bedding spread on the floor.

Parliament: A group of lawmakers in England.

parlor: A room used mostly for conversation and guests, kind of like today's living room—the word comes from the French parler, which means to speak.

perennial plant: A plant that comes back every year, compared to an annual, which dies at the end of the season.

peruke: A wig, like those worn by men in the seventeenth and eighteenth centuries.

petticoat: A woman's undergarment.

Pilgrims: People who make a religious quest over a long distance.

pillory: A wooden frame in which convicted lawbreakers were locked up as punishment.

pomander: A fragrant mixture or clove-studded fruit, carried to combat odors.

port: A place for loading and unloading ships.

printer: Someone who published the newspaper and often acted as postmaster.

privy: An outdoor bathroom facility, also called a necessary.

Puritans: A group of Protestant Christians in England who were persecuted for their beliefs.

Q

Quakers: A group of Christians, also called Religious Society of Friends, who believe in a simple way of life and pacifism.

S

saddler: Someone who crafted harnesses, saddles, and other leather items.

scullery: An outbuilding for dirty work such as laundry and soap making.

shallot: The small boat on a ship used to ferry people to land.

shear: To cut the wool off sheep.

shoemaker: Someone who made and repaired shoes.

silversmith: Someone who made items out of silver like tea sets and candlesticks.

slavery: The act of keeping a person against their will and forcing them to work.

smuggling: Trading forbidden items.

springhouse: An outbuilding constructed over a spring used for keeping food items cold.

stomacher: Part of a lady's clothing, a triangular shaped piece of fabric in the front of a gown.

straw tick: A mattress or pillow filled with dried straw, leaves, grass, or cornhusks.

T

tallow: A mixture of animal fat refined for use in candles.

tankard: A one-handled drinking vessel with a lid.

tavern keeper: Someone who provided meals, drinks, and lodging.

tavern: An inn.

the Orient: The East, as in Asia.

tobacco: A plant that produces leaves that are smoked or chewed.

trencher: A wooden plate used at the table.

tribute: A sum of money or other valuable thing paid by one ruler or nation to another in submission, as the price of peace and protection.

V

Virginia House of Burgesses: The first representative assembly in colonial America.

W

wattle and daub: A method of building that uses twigs, sticks and mud.

weave: To make a fabric by interlacing threads or yarns on a loom.

whitesmith: Someone who made items out of tin like candleholders and foot warmers.

wigmaker: Someone who made wigs.

Bibliography and Resources

Books and Periodicals

Adler, David A. *Benjamin Franklin, Printer*. New York: Holiday House, 2001.

Breig, James. "Early American Newspapering." *Williamsburg: The Journal of the Colonial Williamsburg Foundation*, Spring 2003.

Collier, Christopher, and James Lincoln. *The French and Indian War*. New York, Benchmark Books, 1998.

Crews, Ed. "Spies and Scouts, Secret Writing, and Sympathetic Citizens." *Colonial Williamsburg: The Journal of the Colonial Williamsburg Foundation*, Summer 2004.

Crews, Ed. "Volumes to Last for Centuries." *Colonial Williamsburg: The Journal of the Colonial Williamsburg Foundation*, Summer 2005.

Dolan, Edward F. *The American Indian Wars*. Brookfield, CT: The Millbrook Press, Inc., 2003.

Earle, Alice Morse. *Child Life in Colonial Days*. Stockbridge, MA: Berkshire House Publishers, 1993.

Gray, Edward G. *Colonial America: A History in Documents*. New York: Oxford University Press, 2003.

Hakim, Joy. *From Colonies to Country*. New York: Oxford University Press, 1999.

Hakim, Joy. *Making Thirteen Colonies*. New York: Oxford University Press, 1999.

Hashagen, Paul. "Firefighting in Colonial America" *Firehouse Magazine*, September 1998.

Maestro, Betsy and Giulio. *Exploration and Conquest*. New York: Lothrop, Lee and Shepard Books, 1994.

Slavicek, Louise Chipley. *Life Among the Puritans*. San Diego, CA: Lucent Books, 2001.

Stevens, Bernardine S. *Colonial American Craftspeople*. New York: Franklin Watts, 1993.

Taylor, Dale. *The Writer's Guide to Everyday Life in Colonial America*. Cincinnati, OH: Writer's Digest Books, 1997.

Tunis, Edwin. *Colonial Living*. New York: Thomas Y. Crowell Company, 1957.

Encarta. CD-ROM. Seattle: Microsoft, 2003. (Multiple articles)

Web Sites

University, Museum, and Government Sites

Cape Cod National Seashore http://www.nps.gov/caco/heritage/pilgrims.html

Colonial Williamsburg http://www.history.org/Almanack/life/trades/tradebri.cfm

Fort Raleigh National Historic Site http://www.nps.gov/fora/roanokerev.htm

George Washington's Mount Vernon Estate and Gardens http://www.Mountvernon.org

History of Jamestown http://www.apva.org/history/

Monticello—The Home of Thomas Jefferson http://www.monticello.org

National Park Service (includes information on many colonial-era parks) http://www.nps.gov

National Agricultural Library http://www.nal.usda.gov/speccoll/images1/popcorn.html

National Weather Service Forecast office http://www.crh.noaa.gov/lsx/coop/history.php

The Noah Webster House Museum of West Hartford History
   http://noahwebsterhouse.org/games.html

Northern Illinois University, Blackwell History of Education Collection: Books
   http://www.cedu.niu.edu/blackwell/books.html

Stanley Whitman House http://www.stanleywhitman.org/ropebed.html

Stratford Hall Plantation http://www.stratfordhall.org/ed-servants.html

The Salem Witch Museum http://www.salemwitchmuseum.com

The White House http://www.whitehouse.gov/history/presidents/tj3.html

Privately Held Sites

A Fire Pro http://www.afirepro.com/history.html

Africans in America on PBS http://www.pbs.org/wgbh/aia/part1/1narr3.html

Anne Hutchinson http://www.annehutchinson.com/

Archiving Early America http://earlyamerica.com/lives/boone/

Colonial House on PBS
   http://www.pbs.org/wnet/colonialhouse/print/p-teach_lesson1_answers.html

Mayflower History.com http://www.mayflowerhistory.com/

Native Tech—Native American Technology and Art
   http://www.nativetech.org/games/index.php

Salem Massachusetts Witch Trials http://www.salemweb.com/memorial/

State history guide resources http://www.shgresources.com

World Book http://www2.worldbook.com/

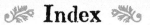 Index

CPSIA information can be obtained
at www.ICGtesting.com
Printed in the USA
LVHW01s2251120917
548425LV00002B/2/P